25 Bicycle Tours on Delmarva

Day Trips and Overnights on the Eastern Shore of the Chesapeake Bay

John R. Wennersten

With the assistance of
Stewart M. Wennersten

Backcountry Publications
Woodstock, Vermont

An invitation to the reader

Although it is unlikely that the roads you cycle on these tours will change much with time, some road signs, landmarks, and other items may. If you find that changes have occurred on these routes, please let us know so we may correct them in future editions. The author and publisher also welcome other comments and suggestions. Address all correspondence to:

Editor, *Bicycle Tours*
Backcountry Publications
P.O. Box 175
Woodstock, Vermont 05091

Library of Congress Cataloging-in-Publication Data

Wennersten, John R., 1941–
    25 Bicycle tours on Delmarva: day trips and overnights on the
Eastern Shore of Chesapeake Bay/by John R. Wennersten, with the
assistance of Stewart M. Wennersten.
        p.   cm.
    ISBN 0-942440-43-9 (pbk.)
    1. Bicycle touring—Delmarva Peninsula—Guide-books.   2. Delmarva
Peninsula—Description and travel—Guide-books.   I. Wennersten,
Stewart M. II. Title. III. Title: Twenty-five bicycle tours on
Delmarva.
GV1045.5.D45W46 1988
917.52′1–dc19   88-9731
                                                                        CIP

Published by Backcountry Publications
Woodstock, Vermont 05091
Printed in the United States of America

Text and cover design by Richard Widhu
Maps by Richard Widhu, © 1988 Backcountry Publications

Acknowledgements

This book has its origins in a series of Sunday afternoon bicycle rides in Wicomico and Somerset counties on Maryland's Eastern Shore. Often I rode with my friend Nat Stelzner. Later, as the book took form, I recruited relatives and friends into making the tours with me.

I am especially indebted to Richard Keenan for accompanying me on two century tours, one of which was made in cold wet weather. Ours was a buoyant enthusiasm that comes only from inexperience.

A number of people gave unstintingly of their time and energy in helping me with the preparation of this book. In alphabetical order, they are: Rick Boston, Don Cathcart, George Demko, Matthew Wennersten, Ruth Ellen Wennersten, and Stewart Wennersten.

My son Stewart helped me with the logistics of the trips and was a constant companion on the tours. My son Matthew came on several trips and cheered us with his jokes.

As in most of my literary efforts, Orlando Wootten has given me great photographic support tempered with an Eastern Shore droll sense of humor. I also owe a special note of thanks to Tom Burton, an expert on the bike routes of the Eastern Shore of Virginia.

Lastly, Ruth Ellen, my wife, put up with my bicycle obsession. She alone knows the value of the 26th tour.

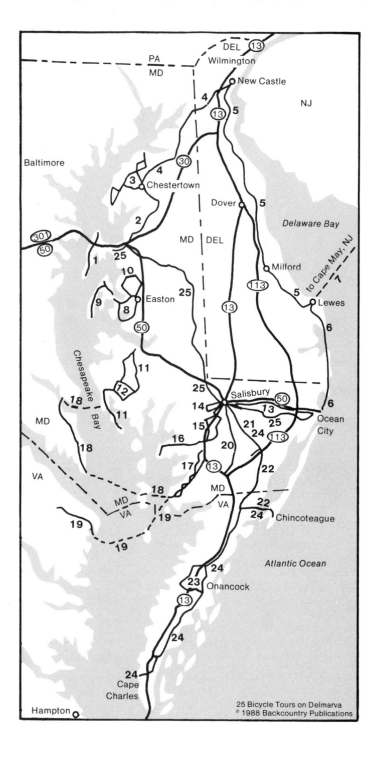

DEL ⑬
PA
MD
Wilmington
New Castle
NJ
4
⑬
5
Baltimore
4
③⓪
3
4
Chestertown
Dover
5
2
Delaware Bay
⓷⓪①
⓹⓪
1 25
MD | DEL
Milford
to Cape May, NJ
7
10
⑪③
5
9
25
Lewes
8 Easton
⑬
6
⓹⓪
Chesapeake Bay
11
25
Salisbury
⓹⓪
6
12
14
⑬
Ocean
18
11
15
21 25
City
MD
16
24 ⑪③
18
20
VA
17
⑬
22
18
MD
VA
MD
19
VA
22
19
24 Chincoteague
19
Atlantic Ocean
19
24
23 Onancock
⑬
24
24
Cape
Charles
Hampton
25 Bicycle Tours on Delmarva
© 1988 Backcountry Publications

Contents

Introduction

The Eastern Shore or Delmarva is a long peninsula lying between the Chesapeake Bay and the Atlantic Ocean. Stretching from Cecil and New Castle counties in the north, the region follows the Chesapeake Bay south to form a diamond of tidewater counties shaped over the millennia by the sand deposits of the Susquehanna River. Three states, Delaware, Maryland, and Virginia, have sovereignty on the Eastern Shore, and the name Delmarva (as the region is popularly referred to) testifies to the social allegiance of its inhabitants.

Until recently the Eastern Shore was isolated from the commercial and metropolitan mainstream of Washington, Baltimore, and Wilmington. Lack of good roads in predominantly rural Delaware prevented commercial penetration of the region. The Chesapeake Bay also isolated Maryland's Eastern Shore population, until the construction of the William Preston Lane Bridge from Annapolis to Kent Island in 1952. The inhabitants of Virginia's Eastern Shore's tightly knit farming community with their time honored ways and local customs often frustrate the cosmopolitan government of Richmond.

On Delmarva look to the water. It is a region defined by the Chesapeake Bay and numerous exquisitely beautiful tidal rivers. Its creeks and snug harbors have provided a livelihood for Chesapeake oystermen and fisher folk since the days of Captain John Smith in the seventeenth century. The region today is a sailor's delight, and cyclists on the Eastern Shore will see watercraft as diverse as giant oil tankers and Chesapeake Bay skipjacks (oyster-dredging sail boats built over a hundred years ago).

Most of Delmarva is flat coastal plain, making cycling on the peninsula an easy ride. South of the Choptank River in Maryland, the countryside is as flat as a pancake. The northern part of the Delmarva Peninsula consists of flat stretches interspersed with gently rolling hills. The most significant obstacle to cyclists on the Eastern Shore is variable winds, especially those out of the south, which can be especially frustrating to the inexperienced cyclist.

Were you to fly over the Delmarva Peninsula in an airplane, you would be struck by the simple fact that the Eastern Shore is the last major green space (over 5,000 square miles) between Boston and Richmond. It is a land of loblolly pine and honeysuckle and fields loaded with grain, corn, and truck produce. Delmarva is also the chicken-producing capital of the Atlantic Seaboard, and the landscape is dotted with thousands of chicken houses that are part of a billion dollar industry. Occasionally while biking you will savor the peculiar aroma of these chicken houses. The poultry industry provides a market for local grain producers and thus contributes greatly to agricultural stability in the region.

The marine climate of the Chesapeake Bay and the Atlantic Ocean makes winters mild. (I have cycled in Ocean City in mid-December in 60-degree weather.) Temperatures rarely plunge below the freezing mark, and except during January and February, it is possible to cycle in all seasons on Delmarva. Summers on the Eastern Shore, however, are ferociously hot and humid, almost subtropical in nature. Cyclists who travel Delmarva in July and August are urged to take precautions against heat stroke. Cycle from dawn till about 11:00 A.M. in summer to make the maximum mileage and avoid the hottest hours. The Eastern Shore also receives an inordinately heavy rainfall (some 49 inches per year), and the squalls of summer and autumn can at times be fierce. Wise cyclists would do well to take training rides in the rain and to pack appropriate rain gear made of fabric that wisks away moisture.

Delmarva, one of the earliest settled areas in the United States, has a rich history. Many farm and seafaring families can trace their ancestry back several generations in the same locale. Pride of birth and heritage are an important part of Eastern Shore life, and local residents like to boast that "a hundred years ain't a very long time on the Eastern Shore." The Delmarva Peninsula is an exquisite gem of Americana. Its gristmills, churches, colonial villages, and small towns offer a vision of America that has all but vanished with the onslaught of metropolitan sprawl surrounding the region.

The Delmarva Peninsula is meant to be savored and explored; it should not be viewed as a physical obstacle to be conquered. The country roads wind leisurely across the rural landscape, and cyclists are largely free from the kind of harassment from motorists that is characteristic of suburbia. "Set a spell," Eastern Shoremen say, a judicious invitation to enjoy the land, its way of life, and its people. Here on Delmarva you can enjoy a crab cake sandwich at a watermen's restaurant in Rock Hall, investigate the colonial architecture of New Castle, or explore the salt marsh expanses of wild Assateague. The Eastern Shore is a magical land of heritage and beauty. Don't hurry. "Set a spell."

Crossing the Chesapeake Bay Bridge

A significant number of cyclists will be approaching the Delmarva Peninsula from Annapolis and the west, using the William Preston Lane Memorial Bridge to cross the Chesapeake Bay. These double spans stride the Chesapeake like behemoths and although it would be a delight to peddle across to the Eastern Shore, cycling is strictly prohibited.

Bicycles in Maryland are prohibited from expressways, certain controlled access highways, and from all toll facilities like the Chesapeake Bay Bridge. The State Department of Transportation, however, recognizes that this prohibition causes problems for long distance cyclists, so the Bridge Transportation Authority offers a courtesy transport service for cyclists. As "time and personnel permit," the Maryland Transportation Authority will carry cyclists over the bridge in a van at the normal car toll. This service, you should note, is a courtesy and not a matter of standard operating policy. If you wish to cross the William Preston Lane Memorial Bridge from Sandy Point (Annapolis) to Kent Island, please phone in advance of your arrival. Contact bridge authorities at (301) 757-6000. Also call ahead when travelling from the opposite direction to make arrangements for a pick-up location and estimated time of arrival.

Chesapeake Bay Ferry Service

One of the truly glorious aspects of biking on the Delmarva Peninsula is riding ferries across the bay to Tangier and Smith islands. Both islands have been inhabited since the seventeenth century, and many of these islanders still speak a vernacular reminiscent of Shakespearian England. So put your bicycle on a boat and go surging across Chesapeake Bay to fishing islands that time has largely forgotten. Also, it is possible to go from Crisfield, Maryland, via Tangier Island, Virginia, to Reedville, Virginia, on the western shore of the Chesapeake. This route is a great way to add some cycling in historic regions of tidewater Virginia to your trip.

Ferry Schedules and Fees

1. *Captain Tyler*—Crisfield, Maryland, to Smith Island, Maryland. Operates daily from Memorial Day to September 30. Departs Somers Cove Marina, Crisfield, 12:30 P.M.; returns 5:30 P.M. 150-bicycle capacity. $21 per person, includes meal. Bicycles are free with fare. Telephone (301) 425-2771.

2. *Captain Jason*—Crisfield, Maryland, to Smith Island, Maryland. Operates each day year round. Departs Crisfield at 12:30 P.M. and 5:00 P.M. Ferry returns to Crisfield at 8:00 A.M. and 4:00 P.M. 150-passenger capacity. $14 round trip. Bicycles permitted. Telephone (301) 425-2351.

3. *Island Belle II* Mail Boat (recommended)—Crisfield, Maryland, to Smith Island and Tangier Island, Virginia. Operates year round. Departs Crisfield at 12:30 P.M. and 5:00 P.M. Ferry returns at 8:00 A.M.and 4:30 P.M. 50-passenger capacity. $5 round trip. Bicycles permitted at a fee of $2 per bike. Telephone (301) 425-4271.

4. *Steven Thomas*—Crisfield, Maryland, to Tangier Island, Virginia. Operates May 1 to October 31. Departs Crisfield 12:30 P.M. Ferry returns at 5:15 P.M. 316-passenger capacity. $14 round trip. $8 one way. Telephone (301) 968-2338.

5. *Captain Evans* — Reedville, Virginia, to Smith Island, Maryland. Operates May 1 to October 15. Departs Reedville at 10:00 A.M. Ferry returns at 4:00 P.M. 150-passenger capacity. $8 each way. $2 fee for each bicycle. Telephone (804) 453-3430.

Points of Interest

The Delmarva Peninsula has a wealth of historic sites, museums, and outdoor parks. Operating hours and fees of many of these attractions vary from year to year, so I have not listed them. Each trip, however, will contain information on all the important points of interest. There is scarcely a town or village on the Eastern Shore that does not have a visible presence that reminds the cyclist of the region's rich colonial and nineteenth-century heritage.

Helpful Hints

Although the Eastern Shore of the Delmarva Peninsula is an easy ride, you should be in good biking shape with the ability to cycle as far as your longest planned day trip. The Eastern Shore is especially popular with the "mature (over age 40) cyclist." The author of this book is 47 years old and has been cycling this region for more than 15 years.

Define your goals for each trip. If you are cycling in a group, make sure everyone agrees on the same goals of mileage, speed, and points of interest.

Reconcile yourself to the fact that you may encounter feisty dogs on your trips. Many otherwise pacific dogs become obnoxious when they spot someone on a bike. You can usually outrun them. If necessary, yell "No!" as loud as you can. This ususally stops them long enough for you to speed away. But sometimes wit and speed fail. In the last case I have had great success using a chemical pepper spray called "Halt." "Halt" is sold in most bike shops and causes no lasting harm to dogs.

Carry a bicycle maintenance book and tools for adjusting the brakes and fixing flats. Carry a tire patch kit, extra tubes, a good bike pump, and first aid materials.

Overestimate the amount of money that you will need. The Eastern Shore is a very popular tourist area, and hotels and motels can be expensive. At the end of each trip I shall identify lodging that I think is a good value for the cyclist.

Avoid the "making distance" syndrome. Stop often, walk away from your bike, bend over and smell the flowers. This activity breaks the monotony of the ride and helps to minimize saddle and hand numbness, the bane of bikers. Eat lightly during breakfast and lunch. When you have finished riding for the day, treat yourself to a hearty evening meal, especially one high in carbohydrates.

A final caution. During the peak summer season, some highways may have large amounts of tourist automobile traffic on the weekend. This is especially true for beach areas like Lewes, Delaware, and Ocean City, Maryland. In summer these areas are best explored during weekdays or in the very early morning.

Always wear a helmet! Your head and personal health are worth the investment. I recommend the Bell Tourlite. I think it is a well-designed and highly protective helmet. Use a helmet that will provide you with the optimum safety and maximum amount of comfort for hot weather use.

Resources

One of the major problems still faced by cyclists, regardless of experience and ability, is locating information on how and where to bike in specific regions. While this book does not pretend to be the final reference text, it does contain some basic information sources that may prove helpful to you.

Maryland
Bicycle Affairs Coordinator, Maryland Highway Administration, 707 North Calvert Street, Baltimore, Maryland 21203, 1 (800) 252-8776.

Delaware
Bicycle Coordinator, Delaware Department of Transportation, P.O. Box 778, Dover, Delaware, 19903, (302) 736-3167.

Virginia
Bicycle Coordinator, Virginia Department of Transportation, 1401 East Broad Street, Richmond, Virginia 23219, (804) 786-2964.

Recommended Books

Tom Cuthbertson, *Anybody's Bike Book,* Ten Speed Press, 1979.
Richard Ballantine, *Richard's Bicycle Book,* Ballantine Press, 1976.
Tom Lieb, *Everybody's Book of Bicycle Riding,* Rodale Press, 1981.

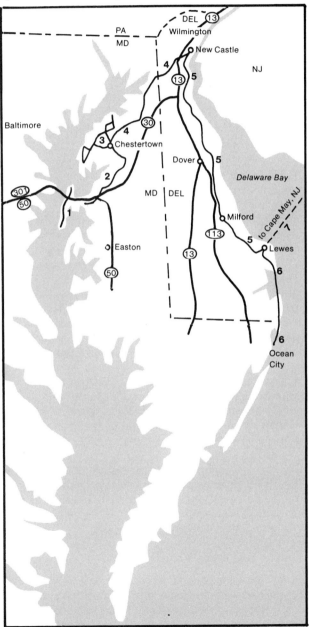

1

Kent Island

Distance: 30 miles.
Terrain: Flat.
Location: Queen Anne's County, Maryland.
Special features: Stevensville, Matapeake State Park, Romancoke, Love Point, views of the Chesapeake Bay Bridge.

Three roads, Route 8, Route 18, and Route 50, form a cross of highways on Kent Island. The principal ride of exploration on Kent Island is the north-south route from Love Point to Romancoke.

Kent Island was settled in 1631 when William Claiborne, a Virginia adventurer, placed a trading post on the island. This was three years before Lord Baltimore's settlers reached St. Mary's. In the seventeenth century, Kent Island was an important center of the Chesapeake fur trade with the Susquehanna Indians who lived to the north. It was also an important prize in the territorial squabbles between the Calvert family and the Virginia colony as to land rights and political sovereignty in the region. William Claiborne and the Lords Baltimore fought in court and intrigued politically for three decades over who had title to and control of Kent Island. The Calverts ultimately prevailed but had to campaign incessantly with lawyers and use the force of arms to win their case.

In the days before the Chesapeake Bay Bridge was constructed, Kent Island was an important auto ferry terminus. Today Kent Island is experiencing metropolitan growth, and the sleepy island of small farms and fishing communities is being transformed by suburban development. On the country roads of Kent Island, weekend automobile traffic can be quite brisk.

Given the geography of Kent Island, it is impossible to make a loop ride. The easiest strategy is to divide the ride into two segments, using Stevensville as a base. After crossing the Chesapeake Bay Bridge, take the first exit to Stevensville. Our ride begins at the parking lot of Stevensville Middle School on Route 18.

Directions for the ride — Romancoke segment

0.0 Stevensville. From the parking lot of the Stevensville Middle School turn left and proceed west on Route 18. Despite growth in the area, Stevensville still retains its Victorian charm. Local churches and fire departments sponsor community suppers, and the island community has an active arts league. Many of the nineteenth-century homes have been restored and are gaily decorated with overflowing flower boxes in summer.

0.6   At the junction of Route 8, proceed cautiously along the Route 50 overpass and continue south on Route 8 towards Romancoke.

1.7   **Christ Church historical marker** commemorates the site of the first Christian congregation in Maryland.

2.3   **Bay City,** one of several small developments on the island, affords a view of Broad Creek and the Chesapeake Bay Bridge.

3.5   **Matapeake State Park.** The state of Maryland has transformed the old ferry terminal into a small but lovely fishing, boating, and picnic area. As you picnic on the shaded grounds of Matapeake, you have a stunning view of the Chesapeake Bay Bridge in the distance. The bridge stands 198.5 feet above the water when it crosses the Chesapeake ship channel and affords ample room for the many freighters that traverse the bay.

The Chesapeake Bay Bridge.

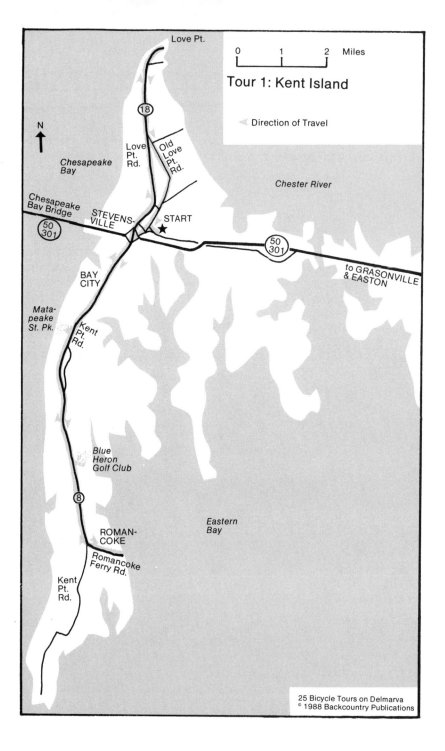

Love Pt.

⑱

Love
Pt.
Rd.

Old
Love
Pt.
Rd.

Chesapeake
Bay

Chester River

Chesapeake
Bay Bridge

STEVENS-
VILLE

START
★

50
301

50
301

to GRASONVILLE
& EASTON

N

BAY
CITY

Mata-
peake
St. Pk.

Kent
Pt.
Rd.

Blue
Heron
Golf Club

⑧

Eastern
Bay

ROMAN-
COKE

Romancoke
Ferry Rd.

Kent
Pt.
Rd.

25 Bicycle Tours on Delmarva
© 1988 Backcountry Publications

6.3   Queen Anne Marina. **Turn right at the Blue Heron Golf Club.** A small marina and restaurant are located here, and one can take light refreshment and spend time at a favorite Chesapeake hobby — boat watching.

9.2   **Romancoke** was once the terminus for a ferry from Claiborne in Talbot County. There is a small park and fishing wharf here at the old terminal site. Out-of-county residents have to pay a fee if they wish to launch their boats here. On a clear day you can easily see the shore line of Talbot County in the southeast.
      Return to Stevensville on Route 8.

Directions for the ride — Love Point segment

0.0   **At the junction of Route 18 and Route 8 proceed north on Route 18.** This is one area of Kent Island still dotted with working farms where the land has not yet been touched by suburban development.

4.3   **Love Point.** Now a quiet village, Love Point was, until 1952, an important terminus for ferries from Baltimore.
      The old ferry wharf is privately owned and is not open to the public. Nevertheless, from Love Point you have a fine view of the bay at the end of Route 18.

6.3   Returning from Love Point, turn left on Old Love Point Road and follow this road into Stevensville.

10.5   Turn left on Route 18 at the Chevron Station. Stevensville Middle School will be on your right.

Lodging
Chesapeake Motel, Route 50 & Route 301, Grasonville, Maryland, (410) 827-7272.

2

Kent Narrows—Chestertown

Distance: 30 miles one way.
Terrain: Flat to gently rolling.
Location: Queen Anne's and Kent counties, Maryland.
Special features: Kent Narrows, Queenstown, Centreville, Chester River, and Chestertown.

This tour is an excellent introduction to the historic towns, villages, and old homes of Maryland's Eastern Shore. You will pass prosperous farms along peaceful country roads that wind lazily north and west through Queen Anne's and Kent counties. Founded in 1706, Queen Anne's County is named for England's Queen Anne (1665-1714), the last of the Stuart sovereigns, whose short reign of 12 years proved to be one of the most successful in English history. Kent County traces its origins to 1658 when it was named by adventurer and fur trader William Claiborne for the estuary of Kent that adjoined Westmoreland County, England.

The county capital of Queen Anne's is Centreville, and, as the name implies, this prosperous little town lies in the center of the county. Proudly perched on the banks of the Chester River, Chestertown is the county seat of Kent, and Chestertown traces its name to the episcopal city of Chester in the English county of Cheshire.

The traffic on the two highways of your journey, Route 18 and Route 213, is pleasantly light. Most tourists follow Route 301 for their auto excursions on this part of the Eastern Shore.

The ride starts at Kent Narrows in the shadow of a large drawbridge that connects Kent Island with the Eastern Shore. Some of the finest yachts in the region pass through Kent Narrows from Eastern Bay in the south to the deeper waters of the Chesapeake. To get to Kent Narrows proceed from the Chesapeake Bay Bridge 2.7 miles to the Kent Narrows drawbridge. At the end of the drawbridge take a sharp right. At the intersection of Route 18 and Route 50 turn right and proceed to the Angler Restaurant (the restaurant is at the end of Route 18 at the water's edge). There are several seafood restaurants with ample parking here, and the Angler Restaurant is open in the morning for breakfast.

From the Angler Restaurant you will proceed east on Route 18 through Grasonville. At 5.3 miles you will come to the intersection of Route 18 and Route 50. As Route 50 is the main thoroughfare to the Atlantic beaches in the summer, use extreme caution when crossing. After crossing Route 50, continue on Route 18 to Queenstown and Centreville. At Centreville you will take Route 213, which leads to the Chester River and Chestertown. The ride across the Chester River Bridge is magnificent as you gaze at the yachts in the river and the mansions that dot the opposite shore.

Directions for the ride

0.0 **Anglers Restaurant.** In summer you can sit at outside tables, have coffee, and watch the great boats pass through Kent Narrows. **Proceed east on Route 18.**

0.6 **Oyster Cove.** This is one of several expensive condominium communities that have recently sprung up in the Kent Island area.

1.2 **Grasonville** is a sleepy town that has a few antique shops and bargain stores. Given its proximity to Annapolis, the town is becoming a commuter suburb.

5.3 **Intersection of Route 18 and Route 50.** After crossing Route 50, you may wish to stop briefly at the Amish Pennsylvania Market. Here the stout, traditional Amish sell a variety of foods brought down from Lancaster, Pennsylvania.

5.6 **At the stop sign turn left. Cross Route 301 and continue onto Route 18 to Queenstown.**

6.1 **Queenstown.** Originally the county seat of Queen Anne's County, the village has a number of fine homes and still has the original courthouse that was built in 1708. Once a thriving port on Queenstown Creek, the town was attacked by the British during the War of 1812. Although tobacco farming and slavery took root here in the seventeenth century, by the American Revolution most farmers in Queen Anne's and Kent had switched to raising wheat and corn.

6.3 **Just outside Queenstown is the lovely St. Luke's Episcopal Church.** Rest on its shady lawn and notice the elaborate Star of David in the large church window.

10.0 **Queen Anne's County 4-H Fairgrounds and birthplace marker of Charles Wilson Peale,** the famous painter of George Washington.

12.6 End of Route 18 and intersection of Route 213. **Turn left into Centreville. Route 213 is divided into two one-way streets through town.**

13.0 **Centreville.** This is a well-kept county seat with many fine eighteenth- and nineteenth-century homes. A market center for the region, Centreville is the kind of pleasant and well-knit country town that would fit into a Norman Rockwell painting. **In Centreville, Route 213 becomes Commerce Street.**

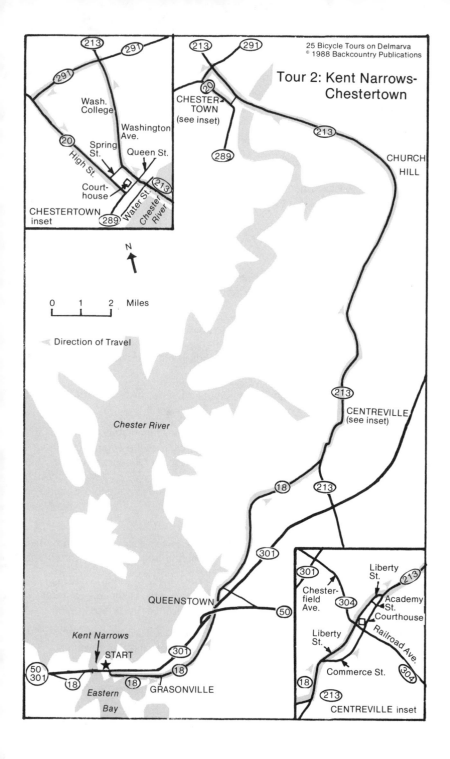

25 Bicycle Tours on Delmarva
© 1988 Backcountry Publications

Tour 2: Kent Narrows-
Chestertown

213   291
213   291
20
CHESTER-
TOWN
(see inset)
213
289
CHURCH
HILL

CHESTERTOWN inset

291   213   291
291
Wash.
College
20   Washington
           Ave.
Spring
St.   Queen St.
High St.
Court-
house
213
CHESTERTOWN   Water St.   Chester River
inset
289

N

0   1   2   Miles

◄ Direction of Travel

Chester River

213
CENTREVILLE
(see inset)

18   213

301

QUEENSTOWN

50

Kent Narrows
START
50
301
18   18
18
Eastern
Bay   GRASONVILLE

CENTREVILLE inset

301   Liberty
      St.   213
Chester-
field   304   Academy
Ave.   St.
                 Courthouse
Liberty   Railroad Ave.
St.
18   Commerce St.   304
213
CENTREVILLE inset

The Court House on the square was completed in 1792 and is the oldest courthouse in Maryland still in use. In the center of the courthouse square you will find a statue of Queen Anne that has recently been installed. Also of interest are the fine Victorian buildings that comprise Lawyers Row parallel to the Court House.

During the Civil War, Centreville was occupied by federal troops because of the rebel sympathies of the local population. Judge Richard Carmichael, a well-known Queen Anne's County jurist, was dragged from his bench and arrested in May 1862, when he attempted to prevent illegal searches and seizures by the Union Army in the town. When he was released from prison seven months later, he received a hero's welcome and resumed his judicial duties.

13.8 **As you leave Centreville on Commerce Street/Route 213, look for Academy Street on your left.** The Academy was the old private school for planters' children. Near the Academy at 202 Liberty Street is a picture-perfect brick house with double chimneys that was built in 1800. Also of architectural interest is Wright's Chance, a gambrel-roofed house built in the 1740s at 119 Commerce Street.

29.0 **Chester River Bridge.** Like most of the country river bridges of the Eastern Shore, this one was built by the WPA during the 1930s. Currently the bridge is in ill repair.

30.0 **Chestertown.** Founded in 1698, Chestertown is the colonial gem of the Eastern Shore. It boasts many fine colonial homes, and High Street and Water Street retain their colonial charm to this day. After crossing the bridge into Chestertown, proceed up Washington Avenue to Washington College. Chartered in 1782, it is the nation's 10th oldest institution of higher learning. Also, it is the only college so named that has a direct association with George Washington. President Washington was a friend of the college, and his portrait by Rembrant Peale, the son of Charles Wilson Peale and a famous artist in his own right, is on view in the administration building.

31.2 **At the intersection of Route 291 and Washington Avenue bear left on Route 291 and loop over to High Street where you turn left again.** This lovely strand has a number of fine shops with colonial-style fronts, a town square with a cast-iron fountain, and a famous Lawyers Row adjacent to the Court House.

Proceed down High Street towards the Chester River. The old Customs House stands on your right at the corner of Front and High streets and dates from the 1730s. During the colonial period, Chestertown was the center of a rich trade in grain, lumber, and molasses with the Caribbean countries.

Near this site on May 23, 1774, irate citizens boarded the sloop *William Geddes* and threw detested tea into the Chester River in protest against the Intolerable Acts of the British government that closed the port of Boston. Each year on a weekend in late May, the town hosts a Tea Party Festival that includes Fife and Drum parades, a reenactment of the *Geddes* tea party, craft fairs, and garden parties. While tourists are a part of local life, they have not overwhelmed the town, and Chestertown continues to be known for its sophistication and good manners.

A note for the return ride

You can return to Kent Narrows via the same route that you took to Chestertown or you can arrange to be met by car or van in Chestertown. As you may not wish to undertake a 30-mile return trip by bike, the second choice seems more practical.

Bicycle repair services
Bikework, 208 Cross Street, Chestertown, Maryland, (410) 778-6940.

Lodging
Foxley Manor Motel, Washington Avenue, Chestertown, Maryland, (410) 778-3200.

Photo by Orlando V. Wootten

Statue of Queen Anne at Queen Anne's County Courthouse in Centerville, Maryland.

3

Chestertown—Rock Hall—Betterton Loop

Distance: 56 miles.
Terrain: Gently rolling to hilly.
Location: Kent County, Maryland.
Special features: Betterton, Rock Hall, views of Chesapeake Bay.

On this tour you are never far from the Chesapeake Bay. Now and then through the trees and across pastures you will have a glimpse of this great body of water. You will travel through some of the prettiest parts of Kent County, Maryland, which contains numerous well-manicured estates and dairy farms. The countryside has a quiet charm reminiscent of England, and I have always been enchanted by its beauty. (I have cycled this loop in both the foulest and best weather and have come away from the tour convinced that this is one of the best bicycle loops on the Eastern Shore.)

Once the rush-to-work traffic to Chestertown ends around 9:00 A.M., the country roads of this part of Kent County are largely deserted. The one exception is Route 20 (the Rock Hall–Chestertown Road), which has a fair amount of afternoon traffic when seafood trucks from Rock Hall rush the day's catch of crabs, oysters, fish, and clams to urban markets.

The ride starts in Chestertown at the intersection of Route 291 and Route 213 and takes you to Betterton via Routes 297, 298, and 292. From Betterton you will travel on isolated back roads south to Rock Hall and from there on Route 20 north to Chestertown.

Directions for the ride

0.0 Start at the intersection of Route 291 and Route 213 (Buzz's Restaurant and Foxley Manor Motel). You may leave your car parked in the restaurant's large lot. Proceed north on Route 213.

1.2 Turn left on Route 297 for Betterton.

3.7 Enter Worton, a small Kent village with a well-kept regional park.

4.8 Turn right on Route 298 (Still Pond Road) at the intersection of Kent County High School.

6.7   Stop briefly to examine "Friendship," a Chesapeake country manor house built in 1782. Continue through the hamlet of Lynch.

8.5   Bear to the left and continue on Route 292 to Still Pond.

9.1   Still Pond is a charming Kent County village with a country store. Many of the Victorian houses have been restored, and the town has much to delight the eye. For centuries local inhabitants believed that Still Pond (now a filled-in marsh) was haunted by the ghosts of the Indians. The name Still Pond derives from nearby Still Pond Creek, which was called Steele Pone Creek on August Hermann's famous Maryland Map of 1673.

9.4   At the junction of Routes 292 and 566 turn left and proceed north on Route 292.

12.1 Enter Betterton. The deteriorated highway that was the bane of cyclists has recently been resurfaced.

13.1 Betterton Beach. In its heyday, before the opening of the Chesapeake Bay Bridge in 1952, Betterton was a well-known Chesapeake Bay family resort that attracted thousands of day-tripping excursionists. Chesapeake steamboats and ferries would leave Light Street in Baltimore at 8:30 in the morning, deposit their passengers at Betterton, and return to the city in the evening. Today this small Edwardian town is a retreat for those who wish to savor bay breezes at one of the local boarding houses and swim and fish in the Chesapeake. The beach and park facilities are well maintained. Walk out on the long jetty and you'll have a nice view of the bay and the bluffs of Betterton. Looking bayward, the large mouth of the Sassafras River is on your right. Plan time for a swim or a picnic on the shady lawns of the park. **As you leave the beach area, take the first right and peddle up Ericsson Avenue, which loops around Betterton. Gear down; this steep hill will test your strength!**

13.7 At the end of Ericsson Avenue turn left on Howell Point Road. This will take you back to Route 292.

13.9 At the stop sign on Howell Point Road turn right on Route 292 south.

16.1 At the fork of Route 292 turn right on Bessicks Corner Road. **Caution:** Bessicks Corner Road is not well marked, so take care not to miss it.

17.7 Turn left at the stop sign and continue on Bessicks Corner Road. Stop at Still Pond Creek Bridge. The creek will be on your right. This is one of the most impressive tidewater creeks on the Eastern Shore. If you did not know that it was an outlet to Chesapeake Bay, you would call it a large lake.

18.8 At the intersection of Bessicks Corner Road and Coopers Lane, Bessicks Corner Road takes two name changes—Still Pond Road and Montebello Road.

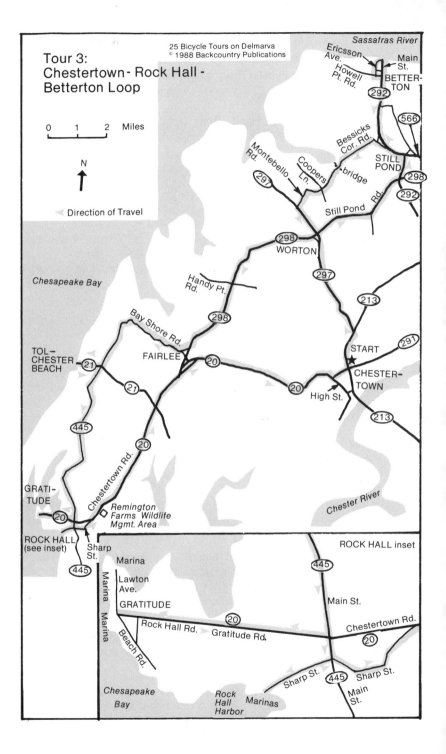

Tour 3:
Chestertown - Rock Hall -
Betterton Loop

25 Bicycle Tours on Delmarva
© 1988 Backcountry Publications

Sassafras River

Ericsson Ave.
Howell Pt. Rd.
Main St.
BETTER-TON
292

0   1   2   Miles

N

Direction of Travel

566

Bessicks Cor. Rd.
bridge
STILL POND
298
292

Montebello Rd.
Coopers Ln.
297

Still Pond Rd.

298
WORTON

297

213

Handy Pt. Rd.

298

Bay Shore Rd.

FAIRLEE

20

START
291

CHESTER-TOWN

213

TOL-CHESTER BEACH
21

21

20

High St.

445

Chestertown Rd.
20

Chesapeake Bay

GRATI-TUDE
20

Remington Farms Wildlife Mgmt. Area

Chester River

ROCK HALL
(see inset)

Sharp St.

445

ROCK HALL inset

Marina
Lawton Ave.
GRATITUDE

445

Main St.

Marina
Marina

Rock Hall Rd.
20
Gratitude Rd.

Chestertown Rd.
20

Beach Rd.

Sharp St.
445
Sharp St.

Main St.

Chesapeake Bay

Rock Hall Harbor

Marinas

Main St.

20.0   At the end of Montebello Road turn left on Route 297.

21.2   Turn right on Route 298.

25.0   At the intersection of Handy Point Road and Route 298 there is a general store, a good place to stop and rest before continuing south to Rock Hall.

28.0   **Fairlee.** Continue through this village and turn right on Bay Shore Road. This route will swing you close to Chesapeake Bay.

32.2   **At the intersection of Route 445 and Route 21, turn right and continue on Route 21 to Tolchester.** Little remains of the once proud resort of Tolchester Beach. Before World War II, however, Tolchester was a premier Chesapeake resort. Owned by the Tolchester Steamship Line, the resort had two hotels, roller coasters, dancing pavillions, and a small lake for boaters. Despite the fenced in look of the place, you are allowed to walk on the beach and swim.

34.2   Return back on Route 21 to the junction of Route 21 and Route 445 south. Turn right on Route 445 south.

39.7   **Enter Rock Hall.** This town, which proclaims to visitors that "nice people live here," is the seafood capital of Kent County. The town's maritime economy provides employment to a small army of seafood dealers, fishermen, oystermen, crabbers, and restaurant and boatyard workers. Named originally "Rock Haul" for the large numbers of rock fish taken here, the town was also an important terminus on the Annapolis to Philadelphia land and water route. Lt. Colonel Tench Tilghman passed through Rock Hall in 1781 as he was taking the news of General Cornwallis's surrender at Yorktown, Virginia, to the Continental Congress in Philadelphia. During the Revolutionary period, Rock Hall was famous for its steamed crabs served at local inns, and Thomas Jefferson and James Madison feasted on them during passages through the area. Today local restaurants continue this tradition.

40.3   **At the intersection of Route 445 and Route 20, turn right on Route 20 (Rock Hall Road).** Notice the large wooden statue of a Chesapeake waterman at the intersection. **Continue on Route 20 to the waterfront hamlet of Gratitude. On your right you will pass a small church called "The Church Mouse."**

41.9   This is a port of entry for Chesapeake yachts and pleasure boats. Spend time exploring the marinas. Return on Route 20 to Rock Hall.

43.5   **Turn right on Route 445, then at the intersection of Route 445 and Sharp Street, turn right on Sharp.** This street will take you to the marinas of the local bay watermen. Stand on the docks and watch the crabbers and clammers unload their catch and joke with one another. If you can, plan to have the daily special of fried soft shell or steamed hardshell crabs at the Watermen's Crab House.

44.5 Proceed back up Sharp Street to Route 445. Turn left on Route 445 and then quickly turn right on Route 20 (Chestertown Road).

47.0 Remington Farms Wildlife Management Area. In 1957, the Remington Arms Corporation took possession of this game preserve, which was formerly owned by Glenn L. Martin, the aircraft millionaire. The preserve has demonstration programs for raising field crops that provide food and cover for geese and ducks. It is open to the public.

56.0 Enter Chestertown on Route 20. Route 20 leads right into Chestertown's famous High Street. Follow High Street to the old Customs House and the wharf of the Chester River and the end of a pleasant loop. To return to your car, proceed up High Street and turn right on Route 291, which will take you to the intersection of Routes 291 and 213 where you began your journey.

Bicycle repair services
Bikework, 208 Cross Street, Chestertown, Maryland, (410) 778-6940.

Lodging
Hill's Inn, 114 Washington Avenue, Chestertown, Maryland (410) 778-1926.

A colonial mansion in Chestertown, Maryland.

4

Chestertown, Maryland—New Castle, Delaware

Distance: 52 miles.
Terrain: Gently rolling with occasional hills.
Location: Kent County, Maryland, Cecil County, Maryland, and New Castle County, Delaware.
Special features: Kitty Knight House, Sassafras River, Bohemia River, Chesapeake City, New Castle.

From Chestertown northward the countryside becomes more rolling and the landscape is dotted with numerous dairy farms. Names on country byways like Clabber Road and Creamery Lane attest to the importance of the dairy industry in Kent County.

Heading north on Route 213, this ride will take you through the Sassafras River country. Named for the tree with its famous medicinal bark, the Sassafras is considered by many to be one of the most beautiful rivers on the Delmarva Peninsula. Unlike the marshy tidal rivers of the southern Eastern Shore, the Sassafras is high banked and well defined. Atop gentle slopes that lead to the water's edge one can spy some of the proudest old estates and plantations in Maryland. Captain John Smith sailed up the Sassafras in 1607 and named it Tockwogh, after the Algonquin Indians who lived here.

During the War of 1812, the Sassafras was an important artery of the grain trade for the American forces. On May 5, 1813, British Admiral George Cockburn sailed up the Sassafras in the HMS *Marlborough* with a flotilla of small boats and 150 marines and burned the twin villages of Georgetown and Fredericktown.

Continuing northward into Cecil County, you will ride across land that once was part of the 25,000-acre Bohemia Manor of August Hermann, the famous seventeenth-century mapmaker. After crossing the Bohemia River, you will soon arrive in Chesapeake City. A delightful village on the Chesapeake and Delaware Canal, Chesapeake City was a thriving canal port in the nineteenth and early twentieth centuries. Nearby is the popular Chesapeake and Delaware Canal Museum.

Crossing the peninsula in a northeasterly direction on back roads, you arrive at the final destination of this tour, New Castle, Delaware. This tastefully preserved colonial center is reminiscent of Williamsburg, Virginia, and was the first capital of Delaware. For two centuries New Castle played an important role in the economy of the Delaware River area.

Directions for the ride

0.0   Depart Chestertown at the Foxley Manor Hotel (where you can leave your car, if you are not having someone drive it to pick you up in New Castle) on Washington Avenue and proceed due north on Route 213.

5.0   **Uriville Pond is on the left.** This is one of the many ponds and lakes created in the region by the New Deal WPA in the 1930s.

7.8   **Kennedyville** is an important dairy center in Kent County and home of a small but thriving Amish community.

10.5   **Historical marker and birthplace of General John Cadwalader,** who was a close friend of General George Washington and a Revolutionary War patriot. When he learned of the "Conway Cabal" to depose Washington from his office, Cadwalader challenged General Thomas Conway to a duel and wounded him in the mouth. Cadwalader subsequently boasted "I have stopped that damned rascal's lying tongue at any rate."

15.3   **Galena.** During the American Revolution Galena was an important way station on the land and water route from Philadelphia to Annapolis. George Washington stopped here on his way to and from the first Continental Congress in 1774. At Galena you will come to the junction of Route 213, Route 290, and Route 313. As you approach the traffic light at the intersection, Billy's Restaurant will be on your right. Turn left at the intersection and continue on Route 213.

17.0   **Kitty Knight House.** Now a famous inn on a bluff overlooking the Sassafras River, the Kitty Knight House is named for an intrepid woman who

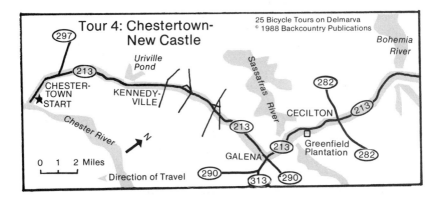

stood up to Admiral Cockburn's invading forces in May 1813. According to local history, Kitty Knight extinguished fires in two houses with her broom as fast as the British soldiers lit them, until a sympathetic officer ordered that these two houses be spared. The rear deck and patio of this inn afford a spectacular view of the Sassafras River.

18.0   **Sassafras River Bridge. Plan to gear your bike down while crossing the bridge, as you will have to climb a steep hill.**

20.0   **Greenfield Plantation.** This estate was patented by John and Mary Ward in 1674. The Georgian mansion that dominates the landscape was built in the 1740s and is a good example of the kind of Chesapeake manor houses that existed in the region before the American Revolution.

20.2   **Cecilton** is a small crossroads hamlet and convenient resting point. Like all the places bearing the name of Cecil in this region, the hamlet of Cecilton was named for Cecilius Calvert, the second Lord Baltimore.

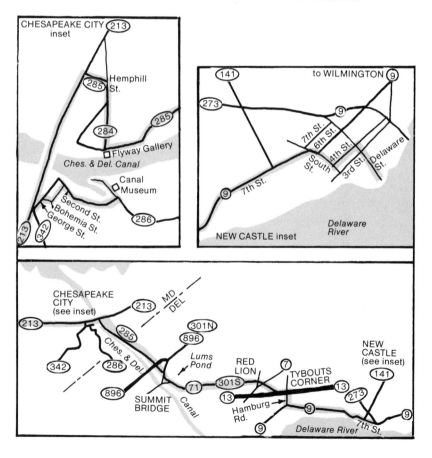

21.8 "The Anchorage," on your left, belonged to the famous Lusby family of eighteenth-century Maryland. This estate was the home of Commodore Jacob Jones and his wife, Ruth Lusby. Jones commanded the United States Naval sloop *Wasp* and was a hero of the War of 1812. The mansion is a fine example of Chesapeake country "telescope" architecture.

24.5 **Bohemia River.** This river is named for the home province of August Hermann, a native of Prague, who settled in Maryland in the seventeenth century. In the 1680s August Hermann was awarded 25,000 acres of land in payment for surveying the province of Maryland. The survey project took nearly ten years, and the August Hermann Map enabled the Lords Baltimore to defend their proprietorship in court against the encroachments of Pennsylvania and Virginia.

30.0 **Chesapeake City. Turn right on Route 286 to South Chesapeake City.**

30.4 **Enter Chesapeake City on George Street and turn right on Bohemia Street. Straight ahead lies the Chesapeake and Delaware Canal. At the intersection of Bohemia and Second Street, turn right onto Second Street to proceed to the Canal Museum.**

31.6 **Chesapeake and Delaware Canal Museum.** The road loops around salt marsh and offers a good view of the canal, Chesapeake City, and the canal bridge. As early as 1661 August Hermann had dreamed of a canal that would connect Chesapeake Bay with the Delaware River, but it was not until 1764 that surveying began. The digging of the canal commenced in 1804, and the canal was formally opened for business in 1829. As the Chesapeake Bay was seven feet higher than the Delaware River, the canal was built with several locks. The old steam engine and waterwheel that pumped water into the first lock are on display in the canal museum. The canal was purchased by the federal government in 1919 and enlarged. Today the Chesapeake and Delaware Canal offers a route that saves Baltimore-bound vessels on the Delaware from the long 400-mile trip down the Atlantic coast and up the Chesapeake.

32.7 **Bridge over the Chesapeake and Delaware Canal.** Traffic is heavy on this narrow bridge, so walk your bike across the high mile-long span on the right-hand sidewalk. For those who are not squeamish, the view from the crest of the bridge of the canal and surrounding area is excellent.

33.8 **At the end of the bridge turn right on Route 285 (Hemphill Street), which will take you into North Chesapeake City.**

34.2 **Turn right on Route 284.**

34.4 **Turn left at the "T" intersection and stop sign onto Route 285. You will be facing the Flyway Gallery. Continue on Route 285, which parallels the Chesapeake and Delaware Canal.**

38.9 A half mile after you ride across the Summit Bridge overpass, turn right on Route 71. This road is an isolated stretch of highway and is not well marked.

39.6 Lums Pond State Park camping area. At this point you will have crossed into Delaware; Lums Pond is the state's largest lake. It was built by the state as a water source for the Chesapeake and Delaware Canal lock pumps. **After Lums Pond State Park, Route 71 becomes Route 301S.**

45.0 Hamlet of Red Lion and junction of Route 7 and Route 301S. Continue north on Route 301S.

46.0 Junction of Route 301S and Route 13 at Tybouts Corner. Turn left on Route 13 north. Route 13 is a busy four-lane highway, so proceed with caution on the shoulder for a half mile.

Photo by Orlando V. Wootten

The author in Chesapeake City, Maryland.

46.7   Turn right at the stoplight intersection of Route 13 and Hamburg Road. Jack's Buffet Restaurant and a gas station will be on your right. Turn right on Hamburg Road and proceed to Route 9.

52.2   Turn left on Route 9. Then continue straight into New Castle on 7th Street. At the intersection of Seventh Street and South Street, turn right on South Street. Turn left on 4th Street, which leads directly to Delaware Street and the heart of historic New Castle.

52.6   New Castle historic area. New Castle, first named Fort Casimir, was founded in 1651 by the Dutch under Peter Stuyvesant. Its location at a bend in the Delaware gave New Castle command of the river traffic. The flags of Sweden, the Netherlands, and Great Britain have flown at the old courthouse near the square. New Castle is also the site where William Penn landed in October, 1682, to accept the New World grant of Pennsylvania from the Duke of York. While many of the old Georgian mansions are in private ownership, several buildings, including the old Court House and Amstel House, are open to the public. **Bike down Delaware Street to the Battery along the Delaware River.** After this long day's ride, you might prefer to take a leisurely walk through this enchanting town. **Note:** New Castle is also a convenient departure point for those who wish to continue into Wilmington and northward into the Brandywine Valley.

A note for the return ride

This tour complements tour 5 and ambitious cyclists may wish to push on to Lewes, Delaware. If New Castle is the end of your journey, plan to be met by car or van. For information about bus service for you and your bike to other destinations, call Greyhound Bus Lines, (800) 528-0447.

Bicycle repair services
The Bike Barn, 500 School Lane, New Castle, Delaware, (302) 328-8975.

Lodging
David Finney Inn, 216 Delaware Street, New Castle, Delaware, (302) 322-6367.
William Penn Guest House, 206 Delaware Street, New Castle, Delaware, (302) 328-7736.

5

New Castle—Lewes

Distance: 89 miles.
Terrain: Gently rolling to flat.
Location: New Castle, Kent, and Sussex counties, Delaware.
Special features: Delaware City, Port Penn, Augustine Beach, Dover Air Base,
  Lewes.

You will find some of the best and worst cycling in southern Delaware on
this trip. Route 9 winds lazily south through the marshes of the Delaware
River, and the nature preserves at Augustine Fish and Wildlife Area and
the Bombay Hook Nature Preserve guarantee that this route will continue
to be one of the loveliest on the Delmarva Peninsula. You can stop and
swim at Augustine Beach or watch birds or the numerous muskrats at
work. In late May and early June the marshes are a festival of color, with
dozens of species of wildflowers in bloom. For the most part, you will be at
peace with yourself on this trip, as Route 9 has little traffic, especially
during the week. The only unwelcome specter on your horizon will be the
Salem nuclear power facility across the Delaware River in New Jersey. Its
ominous presence contrasts starkly with the beauty of Route 9.

Continuing south, you will enter Delaware City, an old canal port with
a restored inn and a battery park overlooking the Delaware River. Once
you pass the village of Leipsic (pronounced "Lipsick" by locals), you will be
in the more trafficked area of Dover. You won't have to look for Dover Air
Force Base; it will be all around you. Planes will be constantly flying
overhead as the base is the home of the Military Airlift Command, the main
troop and transport terminal for the U.S. Armed Forces in Europe. South of
Dover the trip becomes boring, and the principal objective is to get to
Lewes as quickly as possible. Routes 113 and 1 are four-lane highways
that offer a minimally decent shoulder for cyclists. In the summer this will
be the hot part of your trip, so stop often to rest and take plenty of fluids.

One final note: Despite the signs that say "Visit Historic Milford," the
town should be avoided. The traffic patterns are confusing, the roads are
poor, and the town is nondescript. Your time is much better spent on the
beach at Lewes or Cape Henlopen.

Directions for the ride

0.0 **From South Street in New Castle turn left onto Route 9 south.** Leaving

New Castle, the highway is two lanes and heavily trafficked in the morning. **Use caution.**

6.3 On your right you will pass the Occidental Chemical Corporation. Hold your nose and think of the great ride that awaits you.

7.7 At the junction of Route 72 motorists turn right to get out to Route 13 and you will have Route 9 south all to yourself.

9.7 Enter Delaware City. Turn left on Clinton Street and head directly for the Battery Park.

10.4 **Battery Park and Olde Canal Inn.** In the nineteenth century, Delaware was the prosperous eastern terminus of the Chesapeake and Delaware Canal and was also the home port of the Delaware fishing fleet. Delaware City reflected a boom town spirit characteristic of many ports in the Chesapeake Bay region at that time.

By 1917 the town's fate had been sealed by the decision of the U.S. Army Corps of Engineers to construct a new outlet to the canal that would allow for passage of larger ships several miles south of Delaware City. The

Photo by Orlando V. Wootten

The lightship *Overfalls* in Lewes, Delaware.

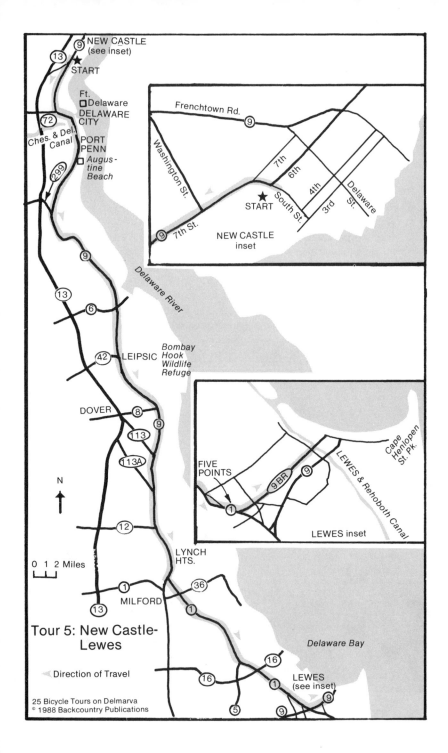

NEW CASTLE
(see inset)
⑬ ⑨
★ START

Ft. ▢ Delaware
DELAWARE
CITY
㉒

Ches. & Del. Canal

PORT ▢ Augus-
PENN tine
Beach
㉙⑨

⑨

⑬

⑥

㊷ LEIPSIC

DOVER ⑧
⑨
⑪⑬
⑬ᴬ

N
↑

⑫

0 1 2 Miles

⑬ ①
MILFORD

Tour 5: New Castle-
Lewes

◄ Direction of Travel

25 Bicycle Tours on Delmarva
© 1988 Backcountry Publications

Delaware River

Bombay
Hook
Wildlife
Refuge

Frenchtown Rd.
⑨

Washington St.
7th
6th
4th
3rd
Delaware St.

★ START South St.
⑨ 7th St.
NEW CASTLE
inset

FIVE
POINTS
⑨ BR ⑨
①
LEWES inset
Cape Henlopen St. Pk.
Lewes & Rehoboth Canal

LYNCH
HTS.
㊱

①

⑯
⑯ LEWES
(see inset)
① ⑨
⑤ ⑨

Delaware Bay

town's canal economy went into decline and Delaware City became a seedy backwater village. Today, however, it has become popular with tourists. The town is undergoing modest gentrification, and the restored Battery Park offers a splendid view of Delaware River. Many people picnic here and spend hours watching the ocean-going vessels heading for Wilmington and Philadelphia.

Historically, Delaware City's principal claim to fame rests on its having been the site of a Civil War fortress and prison camp. Fort Delaware is located on Pea Patch Island in the shipping channel of the Delaware River. Thirty-two-pound sea coast artillery cannons protected the river from Confederate maurading vessels, and the massive stone structure of the fortress is now a museum. Confederate prisoners were housed there during the war.

From the wharf on the old canal near the Battery, you can take a boat out to the fort on the weekends at 11:00 A.M. from late April through September.

You can leave Delaware City either by retracing your route out Clinton Street or by following the road along the old canal (now a favorite mooring site for pleasure boats). Either way, it is a mile back to Route 9 where you will turn left.

Just outside Delaware City you cross a bridge over the Chesapeake and Delaware Canal. On a clear day the view of the canal, the Delaware Bay, and the surrounding countryside is spectacular. On your left from the bridge you will see the current base of the Army Corps of Engineers, which is responsible for maintaining the canal and the ship channels of the Delaware River.

15.1 **Port Penn on the Delaware River lies at the head of Delaware Bay.** Tradition has it that William Penn, the founder of Pennsylvania, once landed there for fresh water. Earlier in this century Port Penn was the home port of an extensive shad and sturgeon fishing fleet. Today it is a charming country village. Stop for hot dogs and coffee at the village market. Also, if time permits, visit Port Penn Museum. **Then continue south on Route 9.**

16.0 **Augustine Beach.** Once a popular resort with bars, a dance hall, and a hotel, today little remains of Augustine Beach. The beach offers good vistas of the Delaware River, however, and is still popular with local fishermen. The beach was named for August Hermann, the famous surveyor of Maryland and Delaware who made a map for Cecil Calvert, second Lord Baltimore, in 1662. In the fall, the wildlife preserve here is filled with thousands of Canada geese.

18.3 **Augustine Fish and Wildlife Area.**

19.0 **Plank bridge across a marsh creek.** The bridge is old and the nail studs are sticking up. To avoid a flat, dismount, and walk your bike across the bridge.

20.9   The colonial mansion "Knowlbush Haven," circa 1780, is one of a few plantations that were built so close to the marsh. Now salt marshes and tidal ponds begin to give way to honeysuckle and corn that sprouts eight feet into the air.

22.7   At the intersection of Route 299 and Route 9, the road forms a "T." Go left on Route 9.

32.0   **Fleming's Landing Bridge.** This bridge in the past has been closed to traffic because of its deplorable condition. It has been repaired recently, however, and it was a pleasure to cross it.

41.0   **Leipsic.** This old fishing and oystering town sits at the edge of the largest tidal marsh area in Delaware. **Cycle through the village,** which is worth a quick visit.

52.4   At the outskirts of Dover Air Base, Route 9 ends. Head south on Route 113.

64.4   **Village of Lynch Heights.** If you do not wish to push on to Lewes, there is a Colony Inn and Restaurant here where you can spend the night.

65.4   **Turn left on Route 1 to Lewes.** Unfortunately, this four-lane ocean highway is the only route you can take. It is a busy road in summer, but there is a wide shoulder to cycle on. **Use caution.**

89.0   Lewes, Delaware. You will enter Lewes at the busy intersection known

An inland waterway in Lewes, Delaware.

as Five Points. Turn left on Route 9BR and proceed into Lewes. Be careful, as there is a lot of traffic in the summer, and vacationers in summer seem to be blind when it comes to cyclists, especially those motorists pulling boats and trailers.

A note for the return ride

For the return trip to New Castle you can either retrace your route by bike or arrange to be met by car or van in Lewes. Considering the distance involved, I strongly suggest the latter alternative.

Bicycle repair services

Bike Etc., 3 North Walnut Street, Milford, Delaware, (302) 422-8030.

Campers Corner/Bike Barn, 500 School Lane, New Castle, Delaware, (302) 328-8975.

Lodging

Colony Inn at Lynch Heights, Route 113 and Route 1, Milford, Delaware, (302) 422-2777.

Cape Henlopen Motel, Savannah and Anglers Road, Lewes, Delaware, (302) 645-2828.

6

Lewes, Delaware—Fenwick Island

Distance: 28.5 miles.
Terrain: Beach dunes and flat highway.
Location: Sussex County, Delaware.
Special features: Lewes, Rehoboth Beach, Delaware State Beaches, Fenwick Island Light House.

For the beach lover, this is the ultimate bicycle excursion. The tour takes you through the lovely seaside towns of Lewes, Rehoboth Beach, and Bethany Beach. These towns are known as the quiet resorts of Delmarva, and you will find little of the tourist pollution, neon, and tinsel characteristic of the Ocean City mega-resort to the south. In fact this trip is designed to end on Fenwick Island at the northern boundary of Ocean City. From there, if you like, proceed south into the traffic-bound expanse of condominiums. My advice is to stay north in Delaware and enjoy the quiet resorts and the still unspoiled state beaches of Delaware. Admittedly there has been some development, especially at Dewey Beach and Bethany Beach, but it has not become grotesque yet.

Lewes, Delaware, has been an interesting coastal spot since Henry Hudson first sailed into Delaware Bay in 1609. In the seventeenth century the Dutch planted a whaling colony on Lewes Creek, and the settlers were massacred by the Indians. Later the Dutch resettled the Lewes area until 1664 when the English gained control of the Delaware colony.

In the past, Lewes was of strategic military importance for it stood at the gateway of Delaware Bay. Since the colonial period, it has been the home of the highly skilled Delaware Bay ship pilots, who help vessels navigate up the Delaware Bay and River to Philadelphia.

Lewes found itself in the crucible of conflict during the War of 1812, and British naval vessels bombarded the town in April, 1813. Throughout the nineteenth century, Lewes was a favorite port for Atlantic coasting schooners. When the railroad came to town in 1869, Lewes became a major fish processing center. Since the 1890s, Lewes has been a small but popular resort. The town is dotted with salt box colonial houses and has a large community of affluent retired citizens. Given the moderate climate, the colonial charm of the town, and access to the beaches of Delaware, property values have skyrocketed.

A short distance from Lewes is Cape Henlopen State Park, a 2,500-acre reserve of surf and sand, seabirds, unusual flora, and winding nature trails. Many cyclists camp at the state campground here, as it is a favorite launching point to catch the nearby Lewes Ferry for Cape May, New Jersey. Throughout the park and along the Delaware coast you will see huge pipe-like towers that dominate the sand dunes. These are World War II bunkers, gun placements, and observation towers. During the war, German submarines were often sighted off the Delaware coast. Today the state has refurbished one of the observation towers in the park, and you can climb the 115 stairs to the top for a grand view of Cape Henlopen State Park and the surrounding beaches.

Directions for the ride

0.0   Given the Dutch antecedents of Lewes, **our trip begins appropriately enough at the Zwaanendael Museum at the intersection of King's Highway and Savannah Road.** You can park your car here. A replica of the Town Hall in Hoorn, Holland, the Zwaanendael Museum was erected by the state of Delaware in 1931 to commemorate the 300th anniversary of the founding of the Dutch settlement here in 1631. The name Zwaanendael means Valley of the Swans, and the leader of the Dutch, David Pieterson de Vries, was born in Hoorn. The museum contains many interesting artifacts that reflect on Lewes' early history.

0.3   **Lewes Historic Complex. From the front of the museum, go left on Third Street.** This will take you to the popular historic complex of colonial homes and shops that have been carefully restored. While many of these structures are private residences, some are open to the public. The Thompson Country Store (built in 1800) is open daily and has a small handicraft and gift shop. **Continue on Third Street to Queen Anne Avenue.**

0.5   **At the stop sign and intersection of Queen Avenue and Third Street, turn right onto Pilottown Road.** In the nineteenth century this area of Lewes was the neighborhood of the Delaware Bay pilots. Today many pilots continue to live in these well-kept Victorian residences.

0.7   **Lewes Public Boat Landing area is on your left, and there is a good view of the town marina and the Lewes–Rehoboth Canal.** The lightship *Overfalls* is moored nearby. Until the 1950s, this boat anchored over Overfalls Shoals off the coast to warn away commercial ships. The lightship is now a museum and is located between Queen and Park avenues on Pilottown Road.

0.9   **Pilottown Road becomes Front Street. Turn left at the traffic light and cross the drawbridge. You will now be on Savannah Road.**

1.4   **Turn right on Cape Henlopen Road and follow the signs to the Cape May–Lewes Ferry and Cape Henlopen State Park.** It is ironic that although Lewes receives ferryloads of motoring visitors every hour, many if not most of these visitors depart quickly, without visiting Lewes or Cape

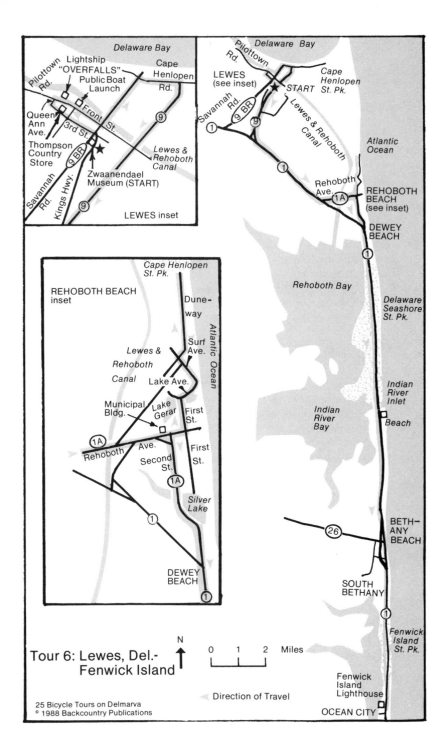

Delaware Bay

Lightship
"OVERFALLS"
Public Boat
Launch

Cape
Henlopen
Rd.

Pilottown Rd.

Queen
Ann
Ave.

Front St.

3rd St.

9

Thompson
Country
Store

9 BR

Savannah Rd.

Kings Hwy.

9

Zwaanendael
Museum (START)

Lewes &
Rehoboth
Canal

LEWES inset

Delaware Bay

Pilottown Rd.

LEWES
(see inset)

Cape
Henlopen
St. Pk.

START

Savannah Rd.

9 BR

9

Lewes & Rehoboth Canal

Atlantic
Ocean

1

Rehoboth
Ave.

1A

REHOBOTH
BEACH
(see inset)

DEWEY
BEACH

1

Rehoboth Bay

Delaware
Seashore
St. Pk.

REHOBOTH BEACH
inset

Cape Henlopen
St. Pk.

Dune-
way

Surf
Ave.

Lewes &
Rehoboth
Canal

Lake Ave.

Atlantic Ocean

Municipal
Bldg.

Lake
Gerar

First
St.

1A

Rehoboth   Ave.

First
St.

Second
St.

1A

Silver
Lake

1

DEWEY
BEACH

1

Indian
River
Bay

Indian
River
Inlet

Beach

BETH-
ANY
BEACH

26

SOUTH
BETHANY

1

Fenwick
Island
St. Pk.

Tour 6: Lewes, Del.-
Fenwick Island

N

0   1   2   Miles

Direction of Travel

Fenwick
Island
Lighthouse

OCEAN CITY

25 Bicycle Tours on Delmarva
© 1988 Backcountry Publications

Henlopen. There are plenty of paved roads in Cape Henlopen, and at the entrances to the beach there are bike racks where you can secure your bicycle.

1.8 Just before entering Cape Henlopen State Park, turn right on Route 9. This will take you west out of Lewes so that you can catch the main road to Rehoboth Beach.

2.4 Cross the bridge on Route 9 over the Lewes–Rehoboth Canal.

4.9 At the traffic light and intersection of Route 1 and Route 9, turn left on Route 1.

8.4 Exit left at the traffic light into Rehoboth Beach. In summer, the traffic is tricky at these intersections and the highway shoulder is often a curse more than anything else. Delaware roads are poorly maintained! **You will know when to turn left to go to Rehoboth when you see the Playland Park and Giant Elephant on your right. So .... turn left at the elephant! You will be on Route 1A.**

9.4 **Rehoboth Beach Municipal Building. Route 1A becomes Rehoboth Avenue.** The town library will be on your right and it's a nice place to stop and rest or browse through a magazine. Directly across the street the Municipal Building offers tourist information. **Proceed straight ahead to the beach and boardwalk.**

Compared to the omni-sprawl and noise of other Atlantic resorts, Rehoboth is civilized, very civilized. But there is evidence of its popularity with nearby metropolitan residents: the beaches may look like volleyball courts and property values have gone out of sight. The town, however, is true to its strict Methodist heritage. Families and children dominate the boardwalk, and the concession stands are fewer in number and less garish than at other resorts. You can bike on the boardwalk in the morning before 10:00 A.M.

Rehoboth Beach is a year-round community that rests comfortably back from the ocean in stands of loblolly pine. The town's name gives it away, for Rehoboth, as taken from the Book of Genesis in the Bible, means "room enough," and there is certainly room enough for cyclists in this resort. Relax and cycle through quiet neighborhoods. Two blocks away from the boardwalk it is hard to believe that you are at Delaware's major resort.

Side Trip: One of my favorite bicycle jaunts in Rehoboth is to head north on 1st Street past Lake Gerar, turning right on Lake Avenue. Then turn left on Surf Avenue. Follow this thoroughfare into Duneway and you will find a very pleasant neighborhood that is close by the sea, yet discreetly tucked away in a pine forest. At the end of the road you will be at the southern boundary of Cape Henlopen State Park.

The town of Rehoboth Beach has more than 15 parks and plenty of lakes and ponds. If you tire of the 1.1-mile boardwalk, there will still be plenty to see and do.

If you are a beach purist and hate crowds, then head south out of town for Delaware Seashore State Park, which contains seven miles of unspoiled beach and facilities for swimming, fishing, camping, and boating. In the off-season you will occasionally see nude bathers here.

9.5   From Rehoboth Avenue head south on 2nd Street. Merge into Route 1A.

10.1   Silver Lake is one of Rehoboth's best fresh water ponds. Given the lush greenery, the bird life, the lake, and the sea, Silver Lake Shores is a swanky development.

12.2   In Dewey Beach, Route 1A and Route 1 merge. After passing through Dewey Beach, home of the summer party and night club set, you will come to Delaware Seashore State Park. The beaches are patrolled by lifeguards, and there are showers, toilets, and ample supplies of fresh drinking water. South of Dewey Beach begins the stretch of Route 1 that will take you cruising for miles along the sand dunes of the Atlantic and the placid waters of Rehoboth Bay.

16.8   Indian River Inlet. Cross the high bridge over the inlet carefully. You'll have a splendid view of the sea and Indian River Bay. Use the sidewalk on Indian River Inlet Bridge; it's safer.

17.6   Indian River Inlet Beach is on your left. Showers and fresh water are available at this guarded beach.

21.6   Turn left into Bethany Beach off Route 1. The street is unmarked, but turn left at the Delaware National Guard and the Exxon Station. Bethany Beach is a good place to stop and rest for lunch.

22.1   At the intersection of Garfield and Pennsylvania streets turn left to go to the beach, or turn right to go back out to Route 1. Turn left (south) on Route 1.

24.7   Fenwick Island State Park. This is the last state beach before Ocean City, so use it to advantage as you will soon be entering the condominium and private beach belt of north Ocean City.

28.3   Turn right on 146th Street to the Fenwick Island Light House. Surprisingly the lighthouse is located on the bay side of the island.

28.5   Built in 1858 to warn ships away from the Fenwick Shoals, the lighthouse was once the largest building at Fenwick. Now the 89-foot structure is dwarfed by high rise apartment buildings. Architecturally, Fenwick Island Light House is one of the best designed structures of this type in the region. Before switching to kerosene in the 1880s, the light burned whale oil.

A note for the return ride

I suggest retracing your path back to Rehoboth Beach, which is exactly what my son Stewart and I did. It is a direct route and relatively free of traffic. However, if you wish, you can continue south on Route 1 to the southern tip of Ocean City and then across Assowoman Bay Bridge and Route 50. Right after the bridge you can pick up the route described from Salisbury in Tour 25 and head west.

In summer, no doubt, you'll be swimming in the Atlantic. Take care to shower well as sand in the critical areas of the body can cause a very uncomfortable ride.

Bicycle repair services

Sundancer, South Baltimore Avenue, Ocean City, Maryland, (301) 289-3516.
Continental Cycles, Inc., 7203 Coastal Highway, Ocean City, Marlyand, (410) 524-1313.

Lodging

Corner Cupboard Inn, 50 Park Avenue, Rehoboth Beach, Delaware, (302) 227-8553 (Expensive but breakfast and dinner are included).
Note: If you wish to spend more than three days in the area, you may be better off renting a condominium from Rehoboth Resort Realty, (302) 227-6116.

The Zwannendael Museum in Lewes, Delaware.

7

Lewes, Delaware—Cape May, New Jersey

Distance: 17 nautical miles across Delaware Bay, 20 miles round-trip cycling in Cape May.
Terrain: Flat to rolling countryside.
Location: Sussex County, Delaware; Cape May County, New Jersey.
Special features: Lewes-Cape May Ferry, Cape May.
Caution: Heavy beach traffic in summer.

This tour will take you off the Delmarva Peninsula and out of Chesapeake Bay country, but the ferry ride across Delaware Bay is so glorious and the town of Cape May so intriguing that the trip is well worth it.

In Cape May you will be able to combine a day at the beach with a tour of the bygone Victorian era. The architecture of Cape May makes it one of the loveliest mid-Atlantic ocean resorts. A National Landmark Town since 1976, Cape May has many "gingerbread" Victorian homes, cottages, and guest houses that lend this resort a distinctive charm lacking in more raucous beach towns like Ocean City.

Cape May is located on a peninsula that stretches some 20 miles seaward. It was an early port for whaling ships, an important commercial fishing center, and it has been a popular summer resort since early in the nineteenth century. The large hotels were the sites of numerous balls for Baltimore debutantes; Wallis Warfield, the future wife of the Duke of Windsor, came out in Cape May.

The Victorian village atmosphere of Cape May also conveys yesteryear's strong sense of family, and Cape May is still very much a family resort. No college high jinks or motorcycle crowds are welcome here! Unlike many resorts, accommodations are reasonably priced. An open-air mall in the center of town is lined with shops and sidewalk cafes. On a summer day, my wife and I spent a pleasant two hours dining and people watching on the mall.

During the tourist season (Memorial Day–Labor Day), Cape May is a chore to navigate on a bicycle. After trying to get through the crowds, my wife and I gave up and parked our bikes in one of the many steel bike racks that are conveniently located. From the mall it is a two-block walk to the beach promenade. Also at the mall the Cape May Historical Society distributes brochures for a historic walking tour of the town. There are more than 600 Victorian houses in Cape May, and as you follow the walking tour, you may find yourself wondering about those nineteenth-century residents who used the hitching posts and carriage steps and gossiped on the large Victorian porches and verandas.

Directions for the ride

0.0   Park your car in the Cape May–Lewes Ferry terminal parking lot at Lewes, Delaware. It is one mile east of the town on the way to Cape Henlopen State Park on Route 9BR. Do not let the large number of cars in the parking lot in summer discourage you; there is always room for a cyclist and a bike on board.

   Purchase your tickets at the outside booths, and line up in the special bike lane. You will probably find yourself among a large group, as the ferry is extremely popular with day-tripping bikers. This is an excellent time to talk shop with cyclists about equipment, places to see and camp, and the joys and problems of the road ahead.

   As you board the ferry you will be directed to park your bike inside the steel bumper lanes. I suggest that you lock your bike to the steel bumper and take your saddlebags with you to the upper decks. This large ferry carries many passengers, and it is better to be safe than sorry. If you are planning to stay only for the day in Cape May, check the ferry schedule. Nothing ruins a relaxing day at the beach like a fast sprint to catch the last ferry back to Lewes.

   The Cape May–Lewes Ferry runs seven days a week, and until September 17 during the tourist season, there is a ferry nearly every hour. Check your ferry schedule for details. The price is moderate: $6.00 each way. For further information, call the terminal in Lewes, Delaware, at (302) 645-6313.

0.0   **Cape May, New Jersey, ferry terminal.** Once you arrive in New Jersey, the ride from the ferry terminal to the town of Cape May is a very uninteresting 5.3 miles. As I travelled this route in summer, I was too preoccupied with traffic to gaze at the landscape; subsequent visits convinced me that I had missed nothing. **From the terminal, follow Route 9 to Cold Spring.**

2.5   **At Cold Spring turn right onto the Seashore Road, Route 626.** It is well marked and the signs are easy to follow. Between Cold Spring and Cape May you will have to cross the Cape May Canal Bridge. It is a bit of a climb, and beach traffic doesn't make it any easier. The road is narrow, so be careful! Also, watch for ruts in the highway.

5.3   The Cape May Seashore Road leads you directly into Broadway, the main thoroughfare that takes you to both the downtown mall area and the beach.

   The easiest way to see Cape May is to **follow Broadway to the beach**

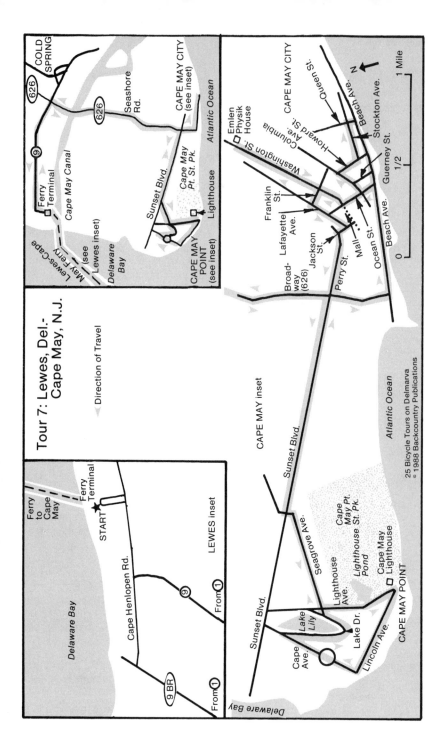

Tour 7: Lewes, Del.-
Cape May, N.J.

▶ Direction of Travel

25 Bicycle Tours on Delmarva
© 1988 Backcountry Publications

LEWES inset

Delaware Bay

Ferry
to
Cape
May

Ferry Terminal

★ START

Cape Henlopen Rd.

9 BR
From 1

9
From 1

COLD SPRING

626

626

9

Ferry Terminal

Cape May Canal

Lewes-Cape May Ferry
(see Lewes inset)

Seashore Rd.

CAPE MAY CITY
(see inset)

Sunset Blvd.

Delaware Bay

Cape May
Pt. St. Pk.

Lighthouse

CAPE MAY POINT
(see inset)

Atlantic Ocean

CAPE MAY CITY

N

1 Mile

Queen St.

Beach Ave.

Stockton Ave.

Howard St.

Guerney St.

Emlen Physik House

Columbia Ave.

Washington St.

Franklin St.

Lafayette Ave.

Broad-way (626)

Jackson St.

Perry St.

Mall

Ocean St.

Beach Ave.

1/2

0

CAPE MAY inset

Sunset Blvd.

Seagrove Ave.

Sunset Blvd.

Cape Ave.

Lake Lily

Lighthouse Ave.

Cape May Pt. St. Pk.

Lighthouse Pond

Lake Dr.

Cape May Lighthouse

Lincoln Ave.

CAPE MAY POINT

Delaware Bay

Atlantic Ocean

and then turn left on Beach Avenue. After one-half mile, turn left on Ocean Street, which will take you into the heart of Cape May's historic district. At 0.3 mile, turn right on Columbia Avenue. On this delightful, tree-lined avenue there are many carefully restored Victorian bed and breakfast inns. At 635 Columbia Avenue you will find the Mainstay Inn, by far one of the most lavish inns in the city. Just off the intersection of Columbia Avenue and Guerney Street is the Gingerbread House, an 1869-styled Victorian cottage with a breezy front porch.

The best way to see it all is to make a loop. **From Columbia, go two blocks and turn right on Howard Street. Turn left on Stockton Avenue, where you are able to see several more Victorian inns.** A favorite with visitors to Cape May is the Victorian Lace Inn, which has spacious rooms and ocean views. Not all of the Victorian homes have been converted into bed and breakfast accommodations; it only seems that way! **On Stockton, go two blocks to Queen Street and turn right. This will take you back to Beach Avenue, where you turn right to complete the loop.**

From Beach Avenue go five blocks to Ocean Street, and continue three blocks to Washington Street. You are now in the mall area; it is best to lock your bike in a nearby rack and continue on foot. **As you come up Ocean Street, the mall will be on your left.** Sample ice cream from one of several sweet shops, find a bench, and watch the parade of vacationers pass by.

Photo by Orlando V. Wootten

The Cape May–Lewes ferry.

No visit to Washington Street is complete without a visit to the old Victorian fire station and museum, which is located one block east from the mall at the corner of Washington Street and Franklin Street. The fire station looks as it did at the turn of the century. Climb upstairs to the small loft and you will be able to see how the firemen slid down the pole to the awaiting engine when fires broke out in Cape May.

If time permits, you will want to visit the Emlen Physick House and Estate, which is located one mile from the mall at 1048 Washington Street in the northeast section of Cape May. Built in 1881, this mansion contains elaborate chimneys, dormers, and trim. It is now a Victorian museum containing a fascinating collection of Victorian furniture, clothing, toys, tools, and memorabilia. It is open to the public daily in the summer and on weekends in spring and fall. The Mid-Atlantic Center for the Arts, P.O. Box 164, Cape May, New Jersey, 08204, sponsors tours of Victorian houses in Cape May from April through December.

If you are a day-tripping cyclist who has put in several hours at Cape May, check your watch. Mind the ferry schedule! There is more to see before you leave.

Backtracking out of Cape May from the Washington Street mall, proceed one block north to Lafayette Avenue. Turn left on Lafayette Avenue and after one block turn right on Jackson Street. Proceed one block to Perry Street and turn left on Perry Street. This will lead you directly out to Sunset Boulevard. Continue straight and head due south for Cape May Point.

It is an easy 20-minute bike ride (three miles) to the Cape May Light House and Cape May Point, a wildlife sanctuary. The present lighthouse has stood guard here since 1859. Nearby Lake Lilly, a body of fresh water, attracts thousands of ducks and shore birds. Cape May Point was originally developed in the 1870s by a group of prominent Philadelphia Presbyterians headed by department store tycoon John Wanamaker.

A note for the return ride

Simply retrace your steps back towards Cape May. From Sunset Boulevard, turn left on Route 626 and out to Cold Spring, where you pick up Route 9 to the ferry terminal.

Bicycle repair services

Shaffers Bike Service, 351 Highway 1 and Red Mill Pond, 4 miles north of Lewes, Delaware, (302) 645-8713.

Hale Bicycle Company, 3–5 Mechanic Street, Cape May, New Jersey, (609) 465-3126.

Lodging

The Gingerbread House, 28 Gurney Street, Cape May, New Jersey, (609) 884-0211.

The Mid-Chesapeake Bay Region

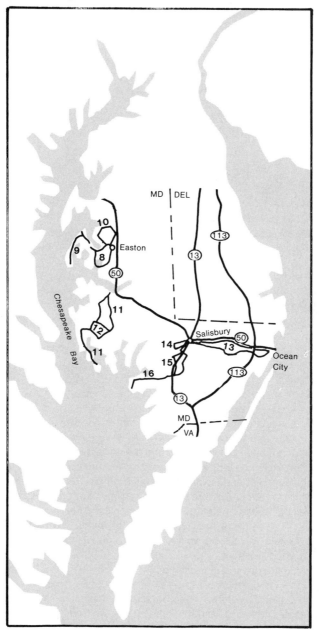

8

Easton—Oxford—St. Michaels Loop

Distance: 31 miles round trip.
Terrain: Flat countryside, one ferry crossing.
Location: Talbot County, Maryland.
Special features: Easton, Oxford, Oxford-Bellevue Ferry, Royal Oak, St. Michaels, Chesapeake Bay Maritime Museum.

This is the kind of trip that both novice and experienced cyclists dream about. The countryside is lovely at any time of year. There are exquisite country towns and villages to explore dating from before the founding of our Republic. The roads are of good quality and have well-marked bike lanes. Thus, you should not be surprised to discover that this is probably the most popular bicycle trip in the Chesapeake Bay country. On all my routes on the Delmarva Peninsula, this is the only tour where I have seen more than seven cyclists at any one time.

Like all trips to attractive historic areas, this one has its drawbacks. Highway 33, the main route connecting St. Michaels and Easton, has heavy traffic on the weekends. Stick well to the side of the road and use caution in crossing the bridge at Oak Creek just before St. Michaels. On the weekends St. Michaels is crowded, and you'll probably have a much better time if you travel mid-week during the summer. Also, this part of the Eastern Shore is stunning in September and October.

Easton is a busy little Eastern Shore town, and its streets can sometimes be a puzzle for the tourist. There are two easy ways to enter Easton. If you are arriving from Route 50 from the north, turn right one mile north of Easton on Route 322. Follow this road for three miles to the intersection of Route 322 and Route 33. Turn left on Bay Street. After 0.3 mile, turn right on Hammond Street. After one block, turn left on Dover Street. This will put you at one of the few free municipal parking lots in Easton. Parking is heavily metered and the meter maids are most diligent in giving tickets to parking violators; hence the elaborate directions in getting you to this lot.

If you are coming to Easton on Route 50 from the south, simply turn left at the intersection of Route 50 and Route 331 onto Dover Street. Follow Dover Street two miles to the municipal parking lot. Another advantage in starting from this area is that you will be right across the street from the Talbot County Library, where the eighteenth-century-styled Maryland Room is well worth a visit.

While some old Eastern Shore towns seem content to bask in the vanished glories of the past, Easton is as vigorous, proud, and pretty as it was in the eighteenth century. Before the American Revolution, Easton was the capital of the Eastern Shore; the difficulties of travel necessitated having two capitals, one at Annapolis, the other on the Eastern Shore. Today Easton wears its mantle easily as the colonial capital, although around the downtown courthouse there are more buildings from the Victorian era than the colonial period.

The Court House Square area is the show piece of Easton, and there are many elegant shops to browse in. The restaurants in the area are nice though expensive. At the Court House you will see a memorial to the Confederate veterans of Talbot County who fought in the Civil War. As many more Talbot Countians fought for the North than the South, this memorial has been a sore point with many local residents over the years. Old disputes die hard on the Eastern Shore!

While you enjoy exploring Easton, watch out for the one-way streets. At the corner of Dover Street and Harrison Street is the famous Tidewater Inn, one of the truly great hostelries of the Eastern Shore. In the inn's restaurant waiters still wear tuxedoes, and the fare is strictly of the Chesapeake region. If you come to Easton during goose hunting season, the lobby of the Tidewater Inn will be alive with the yapping of retrievers since hunters can keep their dogs in their rooms.

Before leaving Easton on the first leg of your journey, be sure to visit the Talbot Historical Society Museum on 29 South Washington Street. Afterwards, continue on South Washington one mile to the Third Haven Quaker Meeting House. This clapboard structure was built between 1682 and 1684 and is one of the oldest wooden frame houses of worship in the United States. During the colonial period, Easton had a significant population of Quakers. After spending a few hours in Easton, prepare to head south to Oxford. The open road awaits you.

Talbot County has always been a wealthy county. In the colonial period it was the heart of the Chesapeake's tobacco empire and in the antebellum period it was the grain capital of the region. Slavery and the plantation style of life died hard here, and many of the fine old manor houses are just visible from the road. Frederick A. Douglass, the famous black orator and abolitionist of the Civil War era, fled from a plantation in Talbot County.

Today Talbot County has become a sailing capital and enclave of some of the richest families in America. The grand manor houses that enabled the old planter class to live and entertain with grace are now owned by corporate chieftains. Talbot has more millionaires per square mile than any other county in Maryland. Small wonder that the county is nicknamed the gold coast.

Directions for the ride

0.0   We begin our journey to Oxford from the municipal parking lot on Dover Street in Easton. From the lot, turn left on Dover Street. At the stop sign turn right on Hammond Street.

0.2   Turn left at the stop sign onto Bay Street.

0.5   At the traffic light turn left on Route 322 for Oxford. You will soon be on Edmundson Neck, a narrow piece of land that juts out into a creek or river. These necks are high and well drained, with access to boat moorings, making them a logical place for the planters to have built their mansions.

1.9   Turn right on Route 333 south. This is the Oxford road.

3.9   Peach Blossom Creek Bridge provides a lovely vista of yachts anchored in the creek.

5.4   Trippe Creek Bridge.

10.6   Enter Oxford. Just before you get into the town limits of Oxford, the Oxford cemetery will be on your right. It is the burying ground of the Tilghman family and other members of the colonial aristocracy who ruled Talbot County in the eighteenth and nineteenth centuries.

Oxford sits comfortably on a peninsula bordered by the Tred Avon and Choptank rivers. During the colonial period, Oxford flourished as a tobacco and shipping center. Its fortunes were linked with the economic exploits of Robert Morris, Sr., who came to Oxford in 1738 as the agent of the Liverpool merchant firm of Foster Cunliffe. Morris made a fortune in tobacco, lumber, and fur trading for his factors in Liverpool and himself as well. His son, Robert Morris, Jr., moved to Philadelphia and played an important role in helping to finance the American Revolution. Understandably, Oxford's main thoroughfare is named Robert Morris Street.

11.5   Robert Morris Inn. Once the residence of Robert Morris, the inn dates from 1774 and has been tastefully restored. The inn overlooks the Tred Avon River and is a stone's throw from the slips of the Oxford–Bellevue Ferry. From the Robert Morris Inn, continue right onto the Strand. This lovely road goes right along side the Tred Avon River, and there are plenty of boats in the harbor to capture your attention.

11.8   Turn right on Mill Street. This will take you past the Oxford Boat Yard and Marina. At the stop sign turn right on Tilghman Street.

12.1   Turn right on Robert Morris Street and return to the Robert Morris Inn and prepare to take the ferry. You may wish to check out the Oxford Mews Bike Boutique that is just up from Clark's Bed and Breakfast Inn at 110 Robert Morris Street. (To get to the boutique and bed and breakfast, turn left at Tilghman Street.)

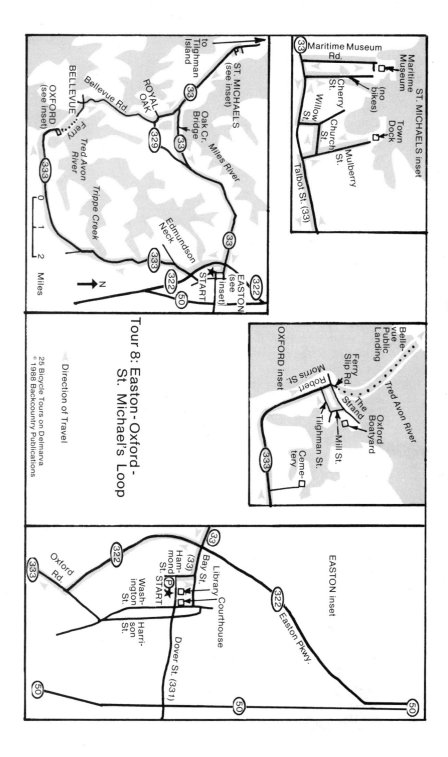

Tour 8: Easton-Oxford -
St. Michael's Loop

25 Bicycle Tours on Delmarva
© 1988 Backcountry Publications

▲ Direction of Travel

12.2 **Oxford–Bellevue Ferry.** My wife, Ruth Ellen, and I crossed the Tred Avon River on a sunny September day. The sky was crystal blue and several large Chesapeake sailboats were coming into port. I gladly paid the boatswain the $1.50 per person toll for a truly majestic river crossing.

12.5 After cycling down the pier from the ferry slip you will enter Bellevue. Once an all black town of cannery and seafood house workers, it is becoming gentrified with vacation estates.

13.0 **Turn right on Bellevue Road.** A road sign points to St. Michaels.

15.9 **After the village of Royal Oak, turn left on Route 329.** Royal Oak boasts a thriving antique emporium and a country store. It is also the home of The Pasadena, a charming country hotel on a tributary of the Miles River. It is a favorite hideaway for Maryland artists and writers.

16.9 At the stop sign you will be at the junction of Route 329 and Route 33. Turn left on Route 33 west.

19.5 **Enter St. Michaels.** Traffic in St. Michaels on the weekends can be heavy. As you proceed down Talbot Street into the village, be careful. Often the gawking tourists are unmindful of pedestrians and cyclists as they drive through town.

Although a certain amount of tourist pollution has affected St. Michaels, it is still one of the most charming villages on the Eastern Shore. The town harbor and wharves are still important entrepôts for Chesapeake watermen, and at various times during the day you can watch them unloading their catches of crabs and oysters on the town dock. Many of the homes in St. Michaels date from the colonial period. To cycle through St. Michaels is to cycle through history. St. Michaels is the oldest town in Talbot County and was a trading center as early as the 1630s.

St. Michaels played an important role in the War of 1812. Here were equipped many of the privateers that preyed upon British ocean-going commerce. According to local history, the shipyards of St. Michaels constructed vessels that were responsible for the capture or destruction of over 500 British merchant ships. So great a threat was St. Michaels, that the British attacked the town on August 9, 1813. The town imposed a blackout, and its shrewd citizens placed lanterns in the trees to misdirect the artillery barrage, thus fooling the British. Only one house was struck, and it is known as the Cannonball House.

In the 1960s St. Michaels awoke from the somnolence of rural life when the Chesapeake Bay Maritime Museum was founded in the town. The museum was dedicated to the lore and history of the Chesapeake, and its attractive and tasteful exhibits made it a mecca for bay country visitors. There is much to learn here about the history of the bay, its traditions in boat building, commercial fishing, yachting, and navigation. A favorite attraction is the 100-year-old Chesapeake Bay lighthouse that was dismantled and brought to the museum. From the museum, you will have a lovely vista of the harbor and the Miles River; and on a bright fall day there may be dozens of sailing craft flying before the wind on the river.

19.9   To explore the town of St. Michaels, turn right on Mulberry Street when you enter the village. This will get you away from the Talbot Street traffic and down to the town dock. At the dock, spend some time watching the watermen or talking to the owners of expensive power boats that are moored here. Mulberry Street is one of the prettiest in St. Michaels. At 200 Mulberry Street is Cannonball House.

20.3   Retrace your way back up Mulberry Street. Turn right on Church Street and take a quick left on Willow Street. This will take you back to Talbot Street, the main thoroughfare, where you turn right.

20.5   Turn right on Cherry Street. There are many old Chesapeake Bay mariner's homes here for you to see. Beware of the signs at the footbridge to the Chesapeake Bay Maritime Museum that say "No Bikes!" To get to the museum, go back out Cherry Street. Turn right on Talbot Street and then right again on Maritime Museum Road. There is a large parking lot for the museum at the end of this lane, and you can park your bike here and visit the museum grounds.

Thomas Point Lighthouse at the Chesapeake Maritime Museum in St. Michaels.

A note on the return ride

When you have fully savored St. Michaels, **retrace your route on Talbot Street out of town to Route 33 east.** (If you continue through St. Michaels on Route 33 west, you will go to Tilghman Island.)

23.9 At the junction of Route 33 and Route 329 east, stay on Route 33 for Easton. Route 329 takes you back to the ferry and Oxford.

24.5 Oak Creek Bridge. Be careful of traffic.

30.4 Junction/traffic light of Route 33 and Route 322. Continue straight through the light on Route 33 into Easton.

30.7 Route 33 becomes Bay Street. Turn right on Hammond Street.

30.9 Turn left on Dover Street into the municipal parking lot.

31.0 Reach the municipal parking lot and the end of your journey.

Bicycle repair services

Bicycles Unlimited, Route 50 north, Easton, Maryland, (410) 822-8666.
Oxford Mews Bike Boutique, 105 South Morris Street, Oxford, Maryland, (410) 820-8222.

Lodging

The Pasadena Inn, Route 329, Royal Oak, Maryland, (410) 745-5053.
Tidewater Inn (expensive), Dover and Harrison Streets, Easton, Maryland, (410) 822-1300.
Robert Morris Inn (expensive), Morris Street, Oxford, Maryland, (410) 226-5111.

9

St. Michaels—Tilghman Island

Distance: 34.1 miles round trip.
Terrain: Flat countryside.
Location: Talbot County, Maryland.
Special features: St. Michaels, Tilghman Island, Claiborne.

You should consider this tour the second part of your trip around the Oxford–St. Michaels area, if you have a few days combine this with Tour 8. As you cycle, remember that you are travelling through one of the oldest areas of Maryland, the ancestral domain of the famous Tilghman and Lloyd families. Proud grain farmers, shippers, entrepreneurs, slaveholders and politicians, the Lloyds and the Tilghmans ruled Talbot County in the eighteenth and nineteenth centuries much like the Cabots and Lodges ruled old Boston. This is also the ancestral land of the famous black abolitionist and social reformer Frederick A. Douglass, who escaped in his youth from the slave-owning Lloyds.

The ride west and south on Route 33 from St. Michaels to Tilghman Island is an easy one. The roads are well marked and there is plenty of highway shoulder. In the fall, however, expect to encounter occasional stiff winds blowing out of the west that will slow you down considerably. But at least you will have the wind at your back for the return trip!

Once you arrive at Tilghman Island, take time to explore. Tilghman Islanders are not the taciturn sort; they like to talk to strangers about their boats and their seafaring way of life. Plan to take your camera as there are plenty of sailing vessels and Chesapeake work boats to photograph.

Directions for the ride

0.0 The trip begins at the parking lot of the Chesapeake Bay Maritime Museum, which is located on Museum Street. There are signs in St. Michaels that point the way to the museum (see Tour 8).

0.2 Proceed down Museum Street and turn right on Talbot Street. Talbot Street will soon become Tilghman Island Road/Route 33.

0.5 Perry Cabin. Now a fashionable Chesapeake country inn and restaurant, Perry Cabin was built before the American Revolution. Greatly expanded in the nineteenth century, it was named in honor of Commodore Oliver H. Perry, the victorious American naval commander on Lake Erie during the

Skipjacks at rest—Tilghman Island.

War of 1812. The inn is open to the public, so you may cycle onto the grounds. Park your bike and walk around to the water side of the inn where you will have an excellent view of the Miles River.

3.4   Junction of Route 33 and Route 451. Bear left on Route 33.

5.0   Wades Point Inn, a local bed and breakfast establishment will be on your right.

7.5   On your right you will be able to see the bay across the cornfields.

12.9 Drawbridge at Tilghman Island. I think this is one of the prettiest spots in Talbot County because it offers a lovely vista of boats of all sizes passing through the Tilghman Island Straits en route to either the bay or the Choptank River.

Just before the bridge on your right is the Bay Hundred Restaurant. In summer, order a refreshing drink and sit out on the veranda and watch the boats pass by. This restaurant is owned by a young couple who are happy to host long-distance cyclists. After resting, **cross the bridge onto Tilghman Island.** You'll find that this little community of fishermen and crabbers is a fairly busy spot. The place is cluttered with piles of wire crab pots and molting sheds for soft-shell crabs.

13.4 Turn left onto the boat ramp and wharf. Much like Deal Island (see Tour 16), Tilghman Island is home port to a diminishing number of Chesapeake Bay skipjacks. These proud sailing vessels continue to dredge the bay for oysters, often in the foulest of winter weather. The skipjacks, which are over one hundred years old and made of wood, have a grace lacking in modern craft. On my last visit by bike to Tilghman Island there were seven skipjacks moored here. Among the prettiest of these was the famous skipjack *Hilda Willing,* owned by Captain Pete Switzer of Tilghman. While at the wharf, you may have a chance to see a boat being rebuilt or overhauled by local shipwrights.

After leaving the wharf, turn left on Route 33 and continue south on Tilghman Island.

13.6 Harrison's Chesapeake House will be on your left. This inn is one of the few remaining Chesapeake Bay resorts left on Maryland's Eastern Shore. Park your bike in the parking lot and walk around the grounds. From here you will have an excellent view of the mouth of the Choptank River. On a clear day you will be able to see Taylors Island in Dorchester County. The inn is a favorite with sports fishermen and duck hunters.

15.0 St. John's Methodist Church will be on your right.

16.1 Blackwalnut Point and Coast Guard Station. You are at the end of the island. From the parking lot you have a good view of Chesapeake Bay, and on a clear day you can see Calvert County on the western shore.

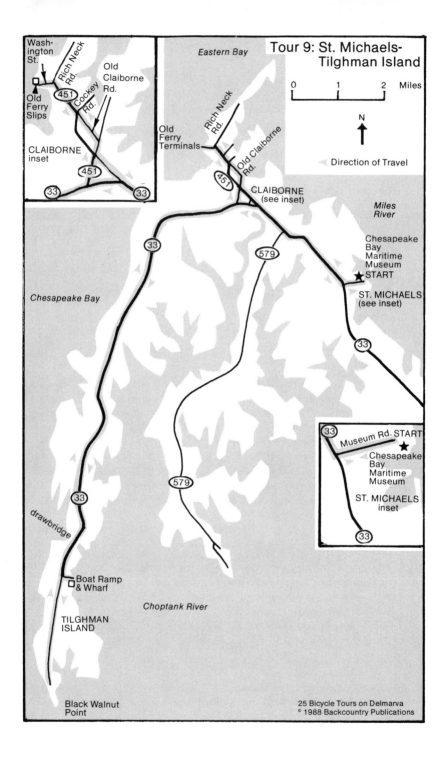

Tour 9: St. Michaels–Tilghman Island

0   1   2   Miles

N

◁ Direction of Travel

Eastern Bay

Rich Neck Rd.

Old Ferry Terminals

Old Claiborne Rd.

451

CLAIBORNE
(see inset)

Miles River

Chesapeake Bay Maritime Museum
★ START

ST. MICHAELS
(see inset)

579

33

33

Chesapeake Bay

579

drawbridge

33

Boat Ramp & Wharf

TILGHMAN ISLAND

Choptank River

Black Walnut Point

CLAIBORNE inset

Wash-ington St.

Rich Neck Rd.

Old Claiborne Rd.

451

Cockey Rd.

Old Ferry Slips

451

33

33

ST. MICHAELS inset

33

Museum Rd. START
★
Chesapeake Bay Maritime Museum

ST. MICHAELS
inset

33

25 Bicycle Tours on Delmarva
© 1988 Backcountry Publications

A note for the return ride

Retrace your route back to the Tilghman Island Bridge and proceed east on Route 33.

28.0 Turn left on Route 451 to Claiborne. A side trip to this village will help to break the monotony of the return ride.

28.5 Turn left on Old Claiborne Road.

29.1 At the intersection of Old Claiborne Road and Cockey Road, turn left, then quickly right on Route 451 and enter Claiborne.

Named for William Claiborne, the English adventurer who established a trading post on Kent Island in the seventeenth century (see Tour 1), the town of Claiborne is today a sleepy Chesapeake hamlet. Before the opening of the Chesapeake Bay Bridge, however, it was an important auto ferry terminal for connections between Talbot County and Kent Island.

One mile outside of Claiborne on Rich Neck Road is Rich Neck Manor, the ancestral seat of the Tilghman family. It was from this plantation that Matthew Tilghman rode to Philadelphia to take his position in the Continental Congress during the American Revolution.

29.6 A right turn will take you up Rich Neck Road to the Tilghman plantation. A left turn on Rich Neck Road will take you to the old ferry slips.

29.8 At the old ferry slips you can see Kent Island straight ahead across the water. The slips are a good place to have a picnic or a swim. After you have relaxed a bit, peddle back on Rich Neck Road and turn right on Route 451.

31.6 At the intersection of Route 451 and Route 33, turn left on Route 33.

33.9 Return to St. Michaels. Turn left on Museum Street.

34.1 Reach the museum parking lot and the end of your loop.

Bicycle repair services

Oxford Mews Bike Boutique, 105 South Morris Street, Oxford, Maryland, (410) 820-8222.

Lodging

Harrison's Chesapeake House, 5831 Main Street, Tilghman, Maryland, (410) 886-2123.

10

Easton–Miles River Loop

Distance: 17.2 miles.
Terrain: Flat to gently rolling.
Location: Talbot County, Maryland.
Special features: Easton, Miles River, Unionville.

This trip complements Tours 9 and 10 and is designed for either the novice or experienced cyclist who wishes to spend a morning or afternoon cycling out of Easton through the countryside of Talbot County. This tour is a perfect Sunday outing, especially after you have had one of those superb brunches at either the Peach Blossom Restaurant or the Tidewater Inn and want to aid your digestion with some low key cycling.

In the fall you can hardly go more than one mile out of Easton before you begin to hear the excited honking of thousands of Canada geese. The fields are full of them, especially on misty mornings. At the opening of goose hunting season, which is usually around the second week of November, over 20,000 people flock to Easton to attend the annual Waterfowl Festival, a three-day show that brings in some of the best waterfowl artists and bird carvers in America to display and sell their work. (For further information on the festival call (301) 822-4567.) If you plan to cycle in the Easton area during Waterfowl Festival time, book a hotel room well in advance.

Directions for the ride

0.0 As in our other loop out of Easton, this tour begins at the Municipal Parking Lot on Dover Street. (See Tour 8 for directions to the parking lot.) Go left on Dover Street out of the lot.

0.1 Turn right on Hammond Street.

0.2 Turn left on Bay Street and proceed to the traffic light.

0.5 Cross Route 322 and proceed west on Route 33 (St. Michaels–Tilghman Island Road).

2.3 Turn right on Route 370. Follow the sign for Tunis Mills–Unionville.

3.0 Within a half mile of each other are two famous Eastern Shore manor houses, Rest and The Anchorage. During the Civil War, the colorful and

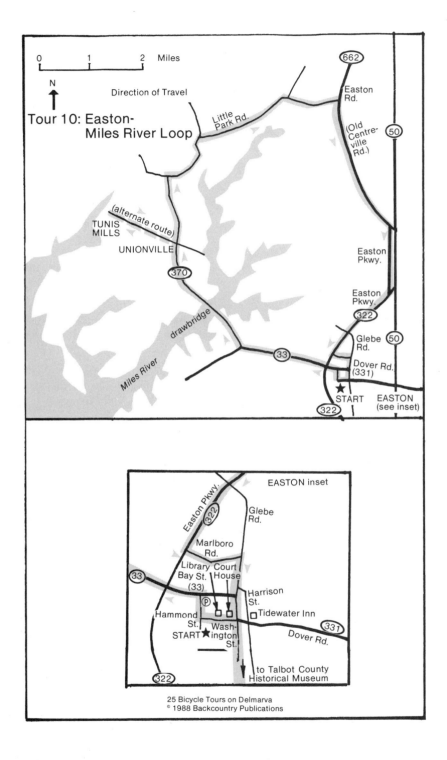

Tour 10: Easton-
Miles River Loop

0   1   2   Miles

N

Direction of Travel

Little Park Rd.

662

Easton Rd.

(Old Centreville Rd.)

50

(alternate route)

TUNIS MILLS

UNIONVILLE

370

Easton Pkwy.

Easton Pkwy.

322

drawbridge

Miles River

33

Glebe Rd.

50

Dover Rd. (331)

START

322

EASTON (see inset)

EASTON inset

Easton Pkwy.

322

Glebe Rd.

Marlboro Rd.

Library Court House

Bay St. (33)

33

Harrison St.

Hammond St.

P

Tidewater Inn

START

Wash-ington St.

Dover Rd.

331

322

to Talbot County Historical Museum

25 Bicycle Tours on Delmarva
© 1988 Backcountry Publications

prominent Lloyd sisters were the mistresses of each plantation. Unfortunately, Sarah Lloyd Lowndes's husband was a Union naval officer, and The Anchorage was in federal territory, while Ann Lloyd Buchanan's husband was a Confederate admiral, and Rest was a Dixie stronghold. During the Civil War, Admiral Franklin Buchanan commanded the iron clad battleship *Virginia* at the Battle of Hampton Roads. He was wounded the day before his ship's celebrated encounter with the USS *Monitor.*

3.1   **When you cross Miles River Drawbridge,** you will have a scenic view of the river and its boat and yacht traffic.

3.4   **The Anchorage plantation.** On your right, close to the shore line, you will see the ruins of St. John's Protestant Episcopal Church. Built in 1839, this was the chapel of the wealthy Miles River gentry who wished to avoid the lengthy trip to church in St. Michaels. You can still see the low crenelated tower; its crumbling walls provide a worthy setting for a Sir Walter Scott novel.

4.6   **Enter Unionville.** This historically black village traces its roots to the Civil War era. St. Stephens African Methodist Episcopal Church will be on your right.

4.9   **Reach the Tunis Mills cut off. You can turn left and enter the sleepy village of Tunis Mills or else continue straight ahead on Unionville Road.** (If you go to Tunis Mills, you will have to come back the same way.)

6.2   **At the stop sign the road comes to a "T." Turn right and follow the sign that says "To Route 50."**

7.4   **The road forks here. Take the right fork and proceed on Little Park Road.** You will quickly come upon a scenic tidewater creek vista on your right. **Note:** Little Park Road becomes Sharp Road.

10.4 **The road again comes to a "T." Turn right at the stop sign onto Easton Road (it is also called the Old Centreville Road/Route 662).** Prepare to climb a hill, which may come as a surprise after miles of flat terrain.

13.4 **Continue on Easton/Centreville Road.** Shortly you will see Route 50 on your left, which runs parallel to the Easton Road. **Continue straight at the stop sign for Easton Municipal Airport.**

14.8 **At the intersection of Easton Road/Route 662 and Easton Parkway, turn right onto the Easton Parkway. Use caution** on the Easton Parkway as the traffic is brisk at times.

15.4 The Black and Decker power tool plant will be on your right.

15.6 At the traffic light, continue straight on Easton Parkway.

16.2 Turn left on Marlborough Road. Tred Avon Square Shopping Center will be on your right. There is no traffic light here, so **use caution** in making a left-hand turn.

16.6 Turn right on Glebe Road.

16.9 Glebe Road becomes Washington Street. Continue on Washington Street into downtown Easton.

17.1 At the Talbot County Court House, turn right on Dover Street.

17.2 Reach the Municipal Parking Lot and the end of your loop.

Bicycle repair services
None on this route.

Lodging
Econo Lodge, Route 50, Easton, Maryland, (410) 822-6330.

Ruins of St. Johns Episcopal Church on the Miles River.

11

Cambridge—Hoopers Island Loop

Distance: 65.7 miles.
Terrain: Flat farmland giving way to marsh.
Location: Dorchester County, Maryland.
Special features: Church Creek, Hoopers Island, Blackwater Marsh.

The trip to Hoopers Island provides an excellent opportunity to see a large portion of Dorchester County, Maryland, and indeed Dorchester is Maryland's largest county. (You can do this tour in conjunction with Tour 12 if you like.) This is tidewater country at its best, and the marshes and small farm communities are tied together through the cycle of nature. The corn fields attract thousands of Canada geese from the marsh. In the early fall mornings the fields are virtually black with these honkers. Thus, Dorchester is a waterfowl hunter's paradise, and many farmers supplement their incomes by leasing duck and goose blinds on their property.

South of Church Creek, the Dorchester landscape turns wild and swampy as you pass through the western corner of Blackwater Wildfowl Refuge. Soon the marsh gives way to the Honga River and you approach Hoopers Island, a prosperous community of watermen and boat builders. Down on the Honga River, the city of Cambridge seems very far away indeed.

Like all marsh routes discussed in this book, avoid this one in summer because of the insects. The best time to take this route is in the fall, when the marsh begins to turn golden brown and thousands of migratory ducks and geese make Dorchester a bird watcher's delight. On this tour, a pair of binoculars will come in handy. It is best to begin this loop at dawn, as the tour requires a full day of cycling.

Directions for the ride

0.0 The trip begins at South Dorchester High School, which is located just south of Cambridge. The school is located at the intersection of Route 16 and Route 343. It is easy to find, and on the weekend you can park your car in the school lot. On weekdays park your car on one of the local side streets in the area. By starting at South Dorchester high school you can avoid the traffic congestion and construction on Route 50. **From Cambridge, take Route 50 south and turn right onto Route 16 for one and a half miles.**

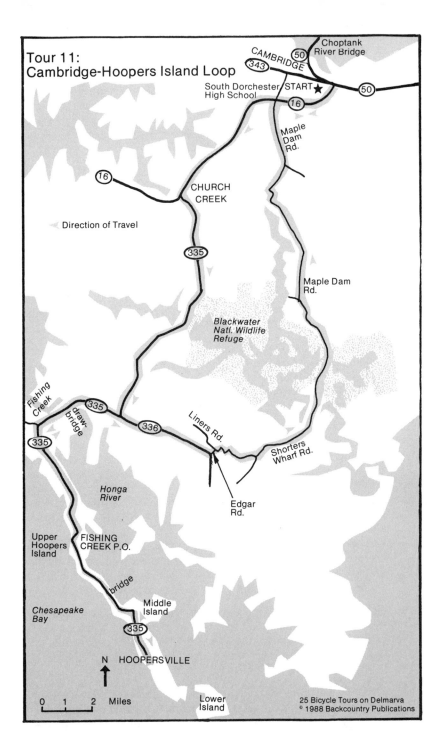

Tour 11:
Cambridge-Hoopers Island Loop

Choptank
River Bridge

CAMBRIDGE 50

343

South Dorchester
High School   START ★

50

16

Maple
Dam
Rd.

CHURCH
CREEK

16

Direction of Travel

335

Maple Dam
Rd.

*Blackwater
Natl. Wildlife
Refuge*

*Fishing
Creek*

335

draw-
bridge

335

336

Liners Rd.

Shorters
Wharf Rd.

335

Edgar
Rd.

*Honga
River*

Upper
Hoopers
Island

FISHING
CREEK P.O.

*Chesapeake
Bay*

bridge

Middle
Island

335

N

HOOPERSVILLE

0   1   2   Miles

Lower
Island

25 Bicycle Tours on Delmarva
© 1988 Backcountry Publications

3.8   **Enter Church Creek,** an old community that developed around Trinity Church in the 1690s. For years, oystering and tomato canneries supported the town, but these days most of the villagers work in Cambridge. Trinity Church itself was built in 1675 and is the oldest church in the United States still in active use. It was restored in the 1960s. (You'll find the church one mile outside the village on Route 16.)

4.8   **Turn left at the Church Creek Post Office onto Route 335.** Now you will be travelling through the Kentuck Swamp and Blackwater Refuge. It is difficult to determine whether Somerset County or Dorchester County marshes are more beautiful. Aubrey Bodine, the famous Maryland photographer, had a definite opinion, however, naming the south Dorchester marsh the most beautiful spot in Maryland. Here you will see vast waving fields of marsh grass and patches of sparkling water that reflect a bright autumn sky. You will want to stop often to gaze at the snow geese and marsh gulls.

14.8 **Come to a crossroads. At the junction of Route 335 and Route 336, turn right on Route 335 towards Hoopers Island.**

18.1 In the midst of this very Protestant countryside, you suddenly come upon **Tubman Chapel,** an eighteenth-century Roman Catholic Church founded by the Tubman family and other Catholics who migrated to Dorchester across the bay from St. Mary's County in the late seventeenth century. This was the site of the first Catholic community in Dorchester County, and today the nearby St. Mary's Star of the Sea ministers to the needs of the small group of Catholics who live here.

21.3 **An old wooden drawbridge crosses Fishing Creek to Upper Hoopers Island.** Hoopers Island is actually a chain of three islands that run parallel to the mainland of Dorchester County. The Honga River estuary will be on your left as you head south. In winter the waters and marshes of the Honga are reported to contain the largest concentrations of wild ducks and geese in the United States.

Originally the island was a farming community, but the relentless encroachment of the marsh and the Chesapeake Bay forced the islanders to turn to the water for a living. Even today you can see areas of land, now salt marsh, that were marked by fence posts for fields and pasture.

22.5 **Fishing Creek Post Office** is the main area of settlement of Hoopers Island. The houses of the village seem to merge with water; backyards face the Chesapeake Bay and front yards face the Honga. Several crab houses operate here, and the village is famed for its steamed crabs. Try lunch at Old Salty's, the only restaurant on the island.

25.1 **Cross the causeway and bridge to the middle island.** The bridge is new, and from its crest you can see all of Hoopers Island. In bad weather the waves from the Chesapeake crash across the causeway.

29.5 **Hoopersville and Rippons Seafood Company.** Hoopersville is strictly a watermen's hamlet, and you can see soft crab sheds where the fishermen deposit their catch of crabs and fish. It is a sparse though tightly knit community.

30.0 **Dead end of Hoopers Island.** The third island has been totally engulfed by marsh. On your left is a privately owned goose hunting club that is replete with its own air-conditioned wine cellar and party rooms.

A note for the return ride

Leave the island and go back out on Route 335.

45.2 Turn right on Route 336.

49.0 Turn left on Edgar Road.

49.3 **Turn right at the stop sign onto Liners Road.** You will encounter one mile of dirt road as you pass through the swamp.

51.0 **Turn left onto Maple Dam Road.** This is a great stretch of highway in autumn as it takes you across the very center of Blackwater Marsh.

65.7 Approach the entrance of South Dorchester High School and the end of the journey.

Bicycle repair services
Bike Shop, 523 Race Street, Cambridge, Maryland, (410) 228-7554 or (800) 660-5860.

Lodging
Econo-Lodge, US Route 50, Cambridge, Maryland, (410) 221-0800.
Commodore's Cottage, Brannock Maritime Museum, 210 Talbot Street, Cambridge, Maryland, (410) 228-6938. (Spend the night in a Chesapeake Colonial Cottage!)

The Methodist Church on Hoopers Island.

12

Blackwater Wildfowl Refuge

Distance: 5.5-mile loop, short tour; 24-mile loop, long tour.
Terrain: Swamp and salt marsh.
Location: Dorchester County, Maryland.
Special features: Blackwater Wildfowl Refuge.

This tour has the distinction of being the shortest and one of the most beautiful bicycle rides that I have written about in this book. As in other rides across the marsh, one rule applies, however: Do not even think about taking this ride in summer. The insects are ferocious and the wildfowl do not even begin to arrive from Canada until October. Therefore, schedule this tour for sometime between late September and the end of November.

Blackwater Wildfowl Refuge is located 12 miles south of Cambridge, Maryland. From Route 50 by car, take Route 16 south to the village of Church Creek. At Church Creek turn left on Route 335. After three miles, turn left on Key Wallace Drive and follow the signs to the visitors parking lot at Blackwater Refuge. The Visitors Center is at the gateway of the refuge and is an excellent starting point for your tour. The center has interesting exhibits about the ecology of the refuge and plenty of tourist information. One caution though, the gate to the parking lot is closed and locked every day at 4:00 P.M.

Since its establishment in 1932 as a refuge for migratory waterfowl, Blackwater has attracted thousands of visitors. Blackwater is one of the chief wintering areas for Canada geese using the Atlantic flyway; at the park's peak in late October or November, there will be about 55,000 geese and 25,000 ducks at the refuge.

If you are serious about combining bird watching with cycling, the best time to visit the park is between mid-October and mid-March. With your binoculars you will see whistling swans, Canada and snow geese, and over 20 species of duck. Though the birds are wild, you will find them nonchalant about your presence. Their sixth animal sense tells them that they will not be harmed at the refuge. There are even traffic signs that warn of goose crossings. My friend George Demko and I cycled through the refuge in late September and we passed within ten feet of large flocks of geese. Out in the fields and farms, however, these honkers won't even let you come within a hundred yards before they take flight!

Blackwater is a very large refuge and retains its primordial wildness. Try to imagine 15,615 acres composed of rich tidal marsh, freshwater ponds, and mixed woodlands. Blackwater is also a haven for endangered species like the peregrine falcon and the Delmarva fox squirrel. Blackwater's importance to me, however, is that it is one of the few places on the Atlantic coast where you can see an American bald eagle in the wild.

Directions for the ride—Short-loop tour

To get to Blackwater Refuge by car, take Route 16 out of Cambridge from Route 50. Head south five miles on Route 16 to Church Creek. From Church Creek, follow Route 335 eight miles to Key Wallace Road. Turn left on Key Wallace Road and follow the signs to the refuge.

0.0   Visitors Center, Blackwater Wildfowl Refuge. Park your car here. Bike out to Key Wallace Road, turn right, and continue to Wildlife Drive.

1.7   Turn right on Wildlife Drive. This is the beginning of the short bike loop through the park. On your right will be the park executive building. Watch out for traffic jams caused by the geese!

2.0   Turn left to go to the observation tower. This 50-foot tower is a must-see on your tour. Climb it to the top and you will have one of the most impressive panoramic views on the Chesapeake shore. The marsh and water stretch off into the vast distance. Heron dive sharply into the water for fish and hawks circle warily alert in the sky. Your best time at the tower

Courtesy of the Maryland Department of Tourism

Canada Geese at the Blackwater Wildfowl Refuge.

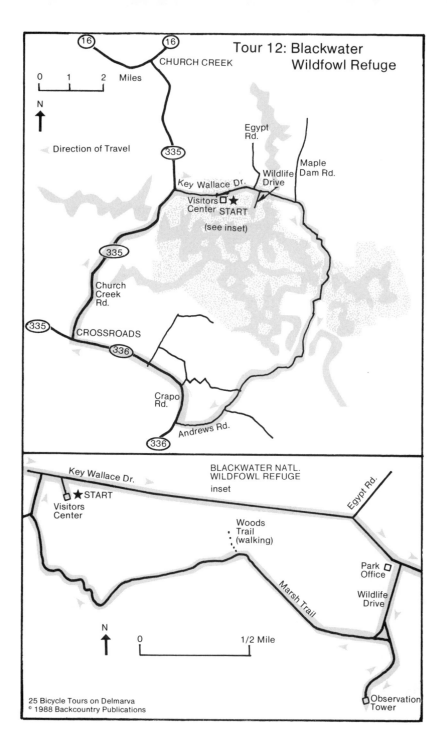

Tour 12: Blackwater Wildfowl Refuge

16 16
CHURCH CREEK

0 1 2 Miles

N

Direction of Travel

335

Egypt Rd.

Maple Dam Rd.

Key Wallace Dr.

Wildlife Drive

Visitors Center ★ START

(see inset)

335

Church Creek Rd.

335 CROSSROADS
336

Crapo Rd.

Andrews Rd.

336

BLACKWATER NATL. WILDFOWL REFUGE
inset

Key Wallace Dr.

Egypt Rd.

★ START
Visitors Center

Woods Trail (walking)

Park Office

Wildlife Drive

Marsh Trail

N

0 1/2 Mile

Observation Tower

25 Bicycle Tours on Delmarva
© 1988 Backcountry Publications

is early morning or sunset when all the birds are roosting in the marsh.

From the tower, retrace your route .25 mile and turn left on the marsh trail. Although it is a designated bike trail, you will share it with automobiles. The trail takes you across the marsh and past fields planted in sorghum, a favorite waterfowl food. It was on this trail that we spotted a bald eagle.

5.2   Turn right at the stop sign onto Key Wallace Road and return to the Visitors Center.

5.5   Return to the visitors parking lot. While you will have hardly broken a sweat on this loop, you will have gotten a bird's-eye glimpse of one of the most impressive waterfowl refuges in America.

Long tour — The Big Marsh Route

Now that the easy loop through the refuge has whetted your appetite for a bigger ride through this 15,000-acre wonderland of water and salt marsh, you are ready for a more adventurous route. Before starting out, check your tools and provisions. Make sure that you have extra tubes, a good bike pump, tools, and water. You will be travelling through the wilds of the south Dorchester County marshlands, one of the most remote areas of Chesapeake Bay country. There are very few gas stations, pay phones, or houses along this route. For most of this loop it will be just you, your bike, and the marsh. Don't throw caution to the winds just because the refuge seems so beautiful and the highway seems so inviting. If you have to walk out of Blackwater Refuge with your bike, it can be a very long walk indeed.

Directions for the ride

0.0   Visitors Center, Blackwater Refuge. From the center parking lot, turn right onto Key Wallace Drive.

1.0   Turn right on Maple Dam Road. Here you will make a long and spectacular crossing of the middle of the refuge and Blackwater Marsh. Out here it is just you, the road, and the wilderness.

3.4   Turn right on Andrews Road.

12.3   Turn right on Crapo Road. This road is Route 336.

21.8   At the hamlet of Crossroads, turn right on Church Creek Road. This is Route 335.

23.0   Turn right on Key Wallace Drive.

24.0   Visitors Center, Blackwater Wildfowl Refuge.

Bicycle repair services
None on this route.

13

Salisbury—Berlin—Ocean City

Distance: 35.4 miles one way.
Terrain: Flat countryside.
Location: Wicomico County and Worcester County, Maryland.
Special features: Salisbury, Berlin, Ocean City.

The trip to Ocean City from Salisbury is an excellent morning's sprint that can easily be accomplished in any season of the year. You will pass through countryside and along highways that, during midweek at least, are deserted country lanes. Even on the weekend in summer, this route is uncrowded and remains the quintessential cyclist's route to the sea. Country hamlets like Powellville still retain their vitality, and country stores are important social centers. Berlin, long chafing under its reputation as a stagnant farm town, is at last stirring. Berlin's business community today is lively and buoyant; hopes in the region are high that the westward expansion of Ocean City's resort prosperity will have a positive impact on local life. Also, Berlin is proud to be the birthplace of Stephen Decatur, one of early America's most daring naval war heroes.

Compared to Berlin, Ocean City is a neon giant that dominates the economy of Worcester County. In winter, Ocean City is a sleepy seaside town of a few thousand. Come summer, however, and Ocean City becomes a teeming resort metropolis hosting more than 225,000 people during any given week. While some visitors may deplore Ocean City's Coney Island atmosphere, others find it the ideal vacation playground. If anything, the resort demonstrates the old axiom that there is no accounting for popular tastes. Ocean City has many facets to its oceanside character. In summer it is a kind of Peter Pan resort, dedicated to the needs and entertainment of the youth of Maryland and beyond. Later, as the tourist season slows around Labor Day, the resort appeals more to families looking for a seaside holiday on a budget. As October looms, the ocean breezes are still warm and large numbers of retirees flock to the resort for what the Ocean City community refers to as "the second season."

Whether it is June or November, Ocean City's mild climate and its surf and boardwalk attract visitors. While Ocean City may not be the resort of your dreams, there is nonetheless something here to appeal to every taste and outlook.

Directions for the ride

0.0   This ride begins at the intersection of College Avenue and Camden Avenue in Salisbury at the campus of Salisbury State College. In summer parking is easily available on side streets near the college, and motels and restaurants are nearby on Route 13 south. Take College Avenue east from the intersection of Camden Avenue and College Avenue. Cross Business Route 13 while continuing on College Avenue, which eventually becomes Beaglin Park Drive.

3.4   Continue to the end of Beaglin Park Drive and turn right onto Mt. Hermon Road/Route 350.

5.4   Pass through the hamlet of Mt. Hermon. At the intersection of Airport Road and Ward's Cash Market continue on Route 350 east through the Wicomico County Nature Preserve. The highway becomes a shady lane and the bird life replaces motor traffic. On both sides of the highway the land becomes spongy, a reflection of the extending swamp and marsh that are so pervasive in the Eastern Shore region.

13.8   Enter Powellville. During World War II Powellville had a large camp of conscientious objectors, some of whom worked on highway construction and swamp drainage projects. Boasting two general stores, Powellville is an excellent place to stop for a cold drink or morning coffee. Adkins Pond, a small dam with a tiny park, is in easy strolling distance of the general stores.

14.4   At the intersection of Route 350 and Route 354, turn right on Route 354.

14.8   Turn left on Route 374. If you miss this turn for Ocean City, you will end up in Snow Hill!

19.5   Pass through the hamlet of Libertytown.

24.1   Enter Berlin. The town's original name was Burleigh, which time and local speech corrupted to Berlin. In the nineteenth century, Berlin was a famous blacksmithing center for the Eastern Shore farm community. The shady winding streets still have many antebellum homes. Of late, this little town has undergone some gentrification. The people here are friendly and the local restaurants are inexpensive and serve good regional fare.

24.9   At Main Street and Farlow's Pharmacy make a sharp right turn. Then quickly bear left at the Peninsula Bank. You will now be on Bay Street/Route 376. Take care not to miss this turn!

25.3   There is a traffic light at the intersection of Route 376 and Route 113. Cross Route 113 and continue on Route 376.

28.8   Ayers Creek. Stop at the bridge and gaze at this large tidal creek with fine

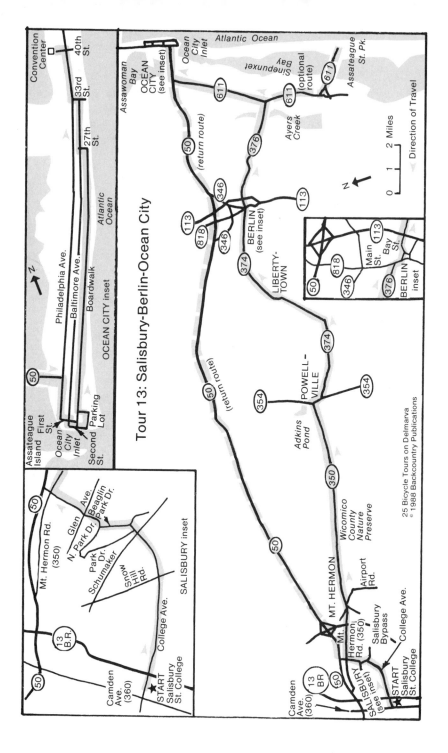

Tour 13: Salisbury–Berlin–Ocean City

25 Bicycle Tours on Delmarva
© 1988 Backcountry Publications

homes perched proudly on its banks. The creek is a favorite with ospreys and sea hawks.

29.5   At the junction of Route 376 and Route 611 you have two options. You can turn right and follow Route 611 to Assateague State Park and its beaches (4.6 miles). There is a public campground at Assateague State Park, though it is often quite crowded in summer. Also, mind the sand flies!

Your other option (the remainder of this tour) is to **turn left on Route 611 and continue onto Ocean City. Caution:** Route 611 is busy in summer, especially where it passes Ocean City Airport.

33.5   At the intersection of Route 611 and Route 50, turn right onto Route 50. **Cross the drawbridge into Ocean City.** Because of the heavy traffic on this bridge, use the sidewalk. The bridge sidewalk is fenced off to protect bikers, walkers, and fishermen from auto traffic.

A sailfish catch in Ocean City, Maryland.

35.4   After the bridge, turn right onto Philadelphia Avenue. Proceed on Philadelphia Avenue to First Street. You are now at the Ocean City Inlet. The
Ocean City Lifesaving Station Museum will be on your immediate left. The
inlet has a fascinating parade of boats going from Assowoman Bay into
the Atlantic Ocean and the Lifesaving Museum has a well-organized
collection of memorabilia on ocean rescue work in the late nineteenth and
early twentieth centuries. Turn left on First Street and follow it into Ocean
City's huge parking lot. The Ocean City Boardwalk begins at the north
end of the lot.

Your experience in Ocean City will be what you make of it. Some see
the resort as the confirmation of their worst fears about resort tackiness in
America. Others are enthralled by the town's boardwalk promenade and
active social life. At this resort you'll see a cavalcade of humanity—from
taffy chewing dowagers to punk motorcyclists with green hair and pierced
noses. Good luck!

Side trip—Boardwalk Minitour

While you are in Ocean City, you will want to bike on the boardwalk to
enjoy the beach scenery and savor the Atlantic breeze. Please note that
you cannot bike on the boardwalk after 10:00 A.M. during the Memorial
Day–Labor Day season. The post season period has less pedestrian
traffic, and you can ride on the boardwalk at any time.

From the inlet parking lot, begin your minitour at the Lifesaving Station
Museum. Proceed up the parking lot towards the giant ferris wheel. Turn
left at Pier Entertainment and right onto the boardwalk. Follow the board-
walk 2.3 miles to its end. From the boardwalk's end go left on 33rd Street.
At the intersection of Baltimore Avenue and 33rd Street, turn right on
Baltimore Avenue. Ride to 40th Street and turn into the mammoth Ocean
City Convention Center. The resort's Visitors and Information Bureau is
located there, and you can obtain literature about all of the resort activities.
Retrace your steps back to 33rd Street and the boardwalk and return to
the inlet parking lot.

A note for the return ride

If you are not going to be met by friends in Ocean City, the easiest way to
return to Salisbury is to take Route 50 west. It is a 37-mile, straight-shot
ride. Though traffic on Route 50 on summer weekends is busy, there is
safe shoulder for you to cycle on. Just be careful!

Bicycle repair services

Continental Cycles, 7203 Coastal Highway, Ocean City, Maryland, (410) 524-1313.

Lodging

Econo-Lodge, 102 60th Street, Ocean City, Maryland, (410) 524-5634.

14

Salisbury Loop

Distance: 13.7 miles round trip.
Terrain: Flat countryside.
Location: Wicomico County, Maryland.
Special features: Salisbury, Pemberton Hall Plantation, Upper Ferry.

This loop is designed to acquaint you with the countryside surrounding the City of Salisbury. Using the city's motels and restaurants as a base, you can spend a delightful weekend cycling virtually in any direction, from Berlin and Ocean City to the east, to Princess Anne in the south.

On this trip you will be cycling primarily through the west side of Wicomico County. Much of your riding will parallel the Wicomico River, and you will have an opportunity to pause along this route and watch the river traffic. Should you desire to cruise on the river, the steamer *Maryland Lady* plies the Wicomico twice a day during the May–September season on luncheon and tourist excursions. Despite Salisbury's urban growth, it is still surprisingly easy to get out into the countryside. On a sunny Saturday afternoon it is great fun to pack a picnic lunch and cycle out of town to the Pemberton Hall Historical Park.

This loop is very popular with racing cyclists who use it as a training run. Expect to be passed every now and then by a group of blazing cyclists! Also, traffic is light on the highways you will be following.

Directions for the ride

0.0 This tour begins at the parking garage on North Division Street in downtown Salisbury. The garage is located across the street from the county library and the town fire station. Easy access to parking makes this an excellent departure point for your tour. To get there, turn off Route 50 at the traffic light onto North Division Street. If you are coming from Annapolis and the west, turn right; if you are coming from the east, turn left.

North-south travellers can enter Salisbury on Main Street at the traffic light intersection of Route 13 and Main Street. If you are coming from the north, turn right on Main Street; from the south, turn left. Proceed one-half mile up Main Street to the "T" and traffic light at the Salisbury downtown plaza. Turn left on North Division Street. The parking garage will be one block on your left.

Once you have parked your car, turn right and proceed back up

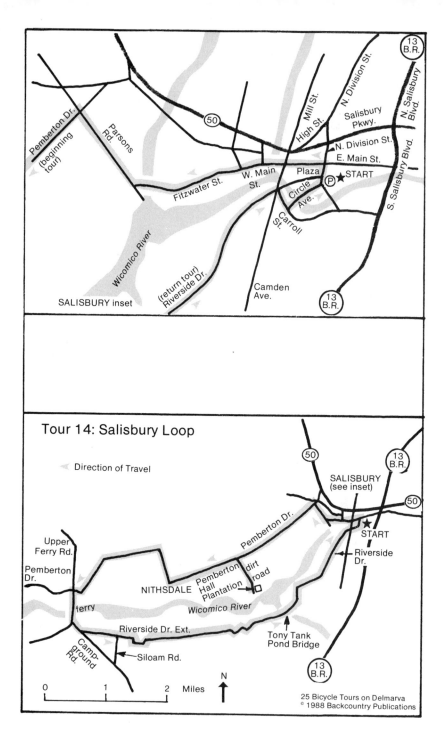

SALISBURY inset

Tour 14: Salisbury Loop

◀ Direction of Travel

25 Bicycle Tours on Delmarva
© 1988 Backcountry Publications

0   1   2   Miles

N

North Division Street to the traffic light and Salisbury Plaza. Once a traffic thoroughfare, the plaza is now an open pedestrian mall with park benches, bubbling water fountains, and tastefully decorated stores. Sorry, biking on the plaza is prohibited, and you will have to walk your bike a short distance.

0.2   At the end of the plaza mount your bike and head straight towards the traffic light. Cross Mill Street and continue straight ahead on West Main Street. You will cross a small drawbridge.

0.4   The entrance to the Port of Salisbury Marina on the Wicomico River will be on your left. This new city-developed marina is the home port of *The Maryland Lady* and a large flotilla of sailing and power vessels.

0.7   Chesapeake Shipbuilding Inc. will be on your left. Salisbury's shipyards played an important role in the economy of the nineteenth-century Eastern Shore. Lately, the founding of this new shipyard has reestablished Salisbury as a center for the construction of Chesapeake vessels. Most of the ships built here are "love boats," cruising vessels for the bay and elsewhere.

1.2   At the stop sign, turn left onto Pemberton Drive. The Shore Stop convenience market will be on your left.

3.15   Pemberton Hall Plantation and Historical Park. To get to the plantation, turn left into the park entrance and proceed down a dirt lane for 0.75 mile. Here you will see a substantial gambrel-roofed brick house built in 1741. The date is on the gable. In the eighteenth century this was the plantation of Isaac Handy and his family. The socially prominent Handys played an important role on the Eastern Shore during the colonial and Revolutionary periods. The architecture of Pemberton Hall has a Flemish quality to it that makes it distinctive in the region. Rescued from near ruin by the dedicated Pemberton Hall Historical Society, the plantation is now a major tourist attraction in Wicomico County. Each October Pemberton Hall hosts a colonial fair that includes music and dancing from the eighteenth century, colonial craft displays, colonial cooking, and horsemanship skills reflective of the Revolutionary era. The plantation has paths, picnic areas, and vistas of the Wicomico River. Go back to Pemberton Drive and turn left.

4.2   Nithsdale will be on your left. Formerly a chicken farm, this area is now a housing development for the newly affluent of Salisbury. It bears the name given to it by a Scottish planter after his native Nithsdale.

5.4   Hollywood Farm will be on your left. Continue on Pemberton Drive.

6.7   At the intersection of Pemberton Drive and Upper Ferry Road, turn left onto Upper Ferry Road.

A colonial fair at Pemberton Hall Plantation.

7.0   Upper Ferry is one of two small cable ferries still working in Wicomico County, and it will give you a short, though delightful, crossing of the river. A ferry has operated here since the colonial period. It derives its name from the fact that it is up-river from the other cable ferry at White-haven on the Wicomico–Somerset County boundary. The ferry has its own idiosyncratic schedule. Between October 1 and February 29, the ferry runs 7:00 A.M. to 5:00 P.M. From March 1 to September 30, the ferry runs 7:00 A.M. to 6:00 P.M. The ferry closes at 1:00 P.M. on Saturday and is closed on Sunday, so plan accordingly. The best part is that the ferry is free.

7.2   After the ferry crossing, the highway forks. Take the left fork onto Campground Road.

7.4   Turn left on Riverside Drive Extension.

8.1   At the stop sign and intersection of Riverside Drive and Siloam Road, keep left onto Riverside Drive.

10.0   Silver Run Community will be on your left.

11.3   Cross Tony Tank Pond Bridge where there is a scenic vista of the Wicomico River.

13.2   St. Francis Catholic Church will be on your right.

13.6   At the intersection/traffic light, turn right on Carroll Street. Then take a quick left at the bridge across a tributary of Wicomico River onto Circle Avenue. Continue up Circle Avenue towards the parking garage.

13.7   At the intersection/traffic light of Circle Avenue and North Division Street, cross North Division Street and enter the parking garage. This is the end of your journey.

Bicycle repair services

Salisbury Schwinn Cyclery, 1404 South Salisbury Boulevard, Salisbury, Maryland, (410) 546-4747.
The Bikesmith, 1053 North Salisbury Boulevard, Salisbury, Maryland, (410) 749-2453.

Lodging

Temple Hill Motel, South Salisbury Boulevard, (.50 mile south of Salisbury State College), Salisbury, Maryland, (410) 742-3284.
Days Inn, Route 13, North Salisbury Boulevard, Salisbury, Maryland, (410) 749-6200.

15

Salisbury—Princess Anne Loop

Distance: 27 miles.
Terrain: Flat.
Location: Wicomico County and Somerset County, Maryland.
Special features: Salisbury City Park and Zoo, Salisbury State College, village of Allen, Princess Anne.

Salisbury, the largest town on Maryland's Eastern Shore, is an excellent base for those cyclists who wish to explore the central Chesapeake. Although Salisbury is rapidly growing as a commercial and medical center, the city retains its small town ambiance. Lawyers and businessmen take long lunches at downtown restaurants, and the pace of life is decidedly unhurried. Salisbury is the seat of Wicomico County, and its location on the Wicomico River has made it an important commercial entrepot since the eighteenth century.

The Newtown area of the city has many fine Victorian mansions and homes that have been tastefully restored. Also, the Salisbury City Park and Zoo offer broad lawns, shady paths, and cool river vistas for tired cyclists. In summer *The Maryland Lady,* a replica of a nineteenth-century Eastern Shore steamboat, regularly plies the waters of the Wicomico River on dining and sightseeing cruises.

Salisbury is also the home of Salisbury State College, a liberal arts school that serves as the town's cultural center. The college houses the Ward Foundation Museum, which is dedicated to keeping alive the Chesapeake Bay folk art of handcrafted duck and goose decoys.

Heading south on your tour, you will pass through the sleepy village of Allen and then directly onto Princess Anne. Still possessing an abundance of colonial charm, Princess Anne is a delight for the American history buff or those who have a fine eye for architecture. Manokin Presbyterian Church on Somerset Avenue dates from 1765, and Somerset County has been the cradle of American Presbyterianism since Reverend Francis McKemie preached in this area of the Chesapeake in the late seventeenth century. Tunstall Cottage at Broad and Church streets dates from 1705 and is the oldest inhabited dwelling in Princess Anne. The town is also the seat of Somerset County, one of the oldest (1666) political units in Maryland.

Prince William Street contains some of the finest antebellum architecture to be seen anywhere in the country. At the head of Prince William

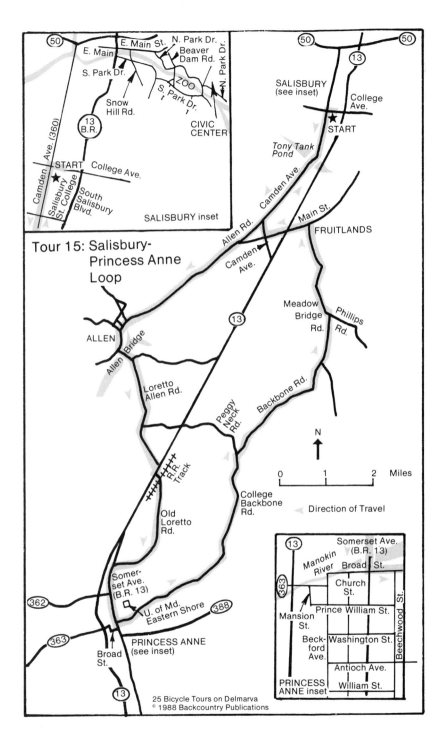

Tour 15: Salisbury-
Princess Anne
Loop

SALISBURY inset

E. Main St.   N. Park Dr.
E. Main   Beaver
Dam Rd.
S. Park Dr.   N. Park Dr.
ZOO
Snow   S. Park Dr.
Hill Rd.
13
B.R.   CIVIC
CENTER
START   College Ave.
Salisbury   South
St. College   Salisbury
Blvd.
Camden Ave. (360)

50   50   50
13
SALISBURY
(see inset)   College
Ave.
START
Tony Tank
Pond
Camden Ave.
Allen Rd.   Main St.
FRUITLANDS
Camden
Ave.
Meadow
Bridge   Phillips
Rd.   Rd.
13
ALLEN
Allen Bridge
Loretto
Allen Rd.
Peggy
Neck
Rd.   Backbone Rd.

N

R.R.
Track
College
Backbone
Rd.
Old
Loretto
Rd.
0   1   2   Miles
Direction of Travel
Somer-
set Ave.
(B.R. 13)
362
U. of Md.
Eastern Shore   388
363
PRINCESS ANNE
(see inset)
Broad
St.
13

25 Bicycle Tours on Delmarva
© 1988 Backcountry Publications

PRINCESS ANNE inset

13   Somerset Ave.
(B.R. 13)
Manokin   Broad St.
River
363   Church
St.
Prince William St.
Mansion
St.   Beck-   Washington St.
ford
Ave.   Beechwood St.
Antioch Ave.
PRINCESS   William St.
ANNE inset

Street stands the sprawling Teackle Mansion with its elegant gardens. Built in 1801 by Littleton Dennis Teackle, a wealthy merchant-planter and associate of Thomas Jefferson, the mansion is a copy of a Scottish manor house.

After touring Princess Anne, stop at the Washington Hotel. This inn has been host to weary travellers since 1744. Afterwards, cycle through the beautiful Georgian-style campus of the University of Maryland, Eastern Shore. I have included an alternate return route map for those wishing to cycle back to Salisbury.

In my opinion, the best time to take this loop is early in the autumn when the weather is cooler and the heat and humidity of summer are but a memory. (**One caution:** you will encounter country dogs on this route, but they are easily handled by experienced cyclists. See my section on dog psychology in the Introduction.)

Directions for the ride

0.0   This tour begins at the entrance of Salisbury State College on Camden Avenue. Ample parking is available on side streets and motel accommodations are close by. **From Salisbury State College head south on Camden Avenue.**

1.0   On both your right and left observe the large ponds created by the New Deal WPA in the 1930s. You are now at Tony Tank, a site that bears the corruption of an old Algonquin name now lost to history. Notice the restored colonnaded late nineteenth-century mansion on your right. Tony Tank is currently an affluent enclave for the elite of Salisbury. You may wish to turn right on Tony Tank Lane and sample the wooded atmosphere of this quiet neighborhood.

2.5   Turn right off Camden Avenue onto the Allen Road cutoff. The Farm House Tavern will be on your right.

6.1   Enter the village of Allen, a quaint hamlet located on the boundary of Wicomico and Somerset counties. Allen traces its settlement to 1667. Many of the clapboard houses have been restored, including Virgina Cottage, a well-known colonial manor house that will be on your left as you cycle through Allen. While at Allen, stop at the Allen Post Office and Country Store, a remnant of the kind of country stores that prevailed in the Chesapeake country in the 1930s. It is a good place to replenish supplies and liquids, and many cyclists stop here enroute to Princess Anne.

6.8   Allen Bridge. Here you have a good view of a large dammed pond that is a delight for weekend fishermen. It is a good place to stop for a picnic lunch. **Shortly after the bridge the road forks. Continue right on Loretto Allen Road.**

9.6 At the intersection of Allen Road and Route 13, cross Route 13 and proceed across railroad tracks onto Old Loretto Road, which will take you to the outskirts of Princess Anne.

12.2 Turn left at the stop sign onto Somerset Avenue (also known as Business Route 13).

13.3 Manokin Presbyterian Church will be on your right.

13.5 The intersection of Somerset Avenue and Broad Street (traffic light) marks the downtown area of the village of Princess Anne. Spend some time touring Princess Anne.

A note for the return ride

13.5 At the intersection and traffic light on Somerset Avenue and Broad Sreet in Princess Anne, turn left and head east on University Drive towards the University of Maryland, Eastern Shore. Originally founded in 1886 as Princess Anne Academy, an industrial and agricultural training institute for blacks, the University of Maryland, Eastern Shore, is now an

Photo by Orlando V. Wootten

Campus of the University of Maryland, Eastern Shore, in Princess Anne, Maryland.

important undergraduate and research component of the University of Maryland system. The campus is nationally known for its research on crops, poultry, nutrition, and Chesapeake Bay marine science. If you do not wish to enter the campus, turn left at the stop sign onto the university loop. If you cross the campus, enter the quadrangle. At the library rejoin the service road to the campus farm.

14.3   At the stop sign the loop ends at the University of Maryland Agricultural Teaching Center and campus farm. Turn left at the stop sign onto College Backbone Road.

18.5   The junction of Peggy Neck Road, College Backbone Road, and Backbone Road is confusing. Examine the signs carefully and make sure that you turn right onto Backbone Road.

21.3   At the stop sign turn left off of Backbone Road onto Meadowbridge Road.

22.3   At the intersection of Phillips Road and Meadowbridge Road, keep left on Meadowbridge Road.

24.0   Meadowbridge Road merges with East Main Street in the town of Fruitland.

24.6   At the intersection of Main Street and Route 13, cross Route 13 and continue on West Main Street.

25.0   At the intersection and flashing light at West Main Street and Camden Avenue, turn right on Camden Avenue.

27.0   Approach the entrance of Salisbury State College and the end of your tour.

Bicycle repair services
Salisbury Schwinn, 1404 South Salisbury Blvd., Salisbury, Maryland, (410) 546-4747.

Lodging
Washington Hotel, Somerset Avenue, Princess Anne, Maryland, (410) 651-2525.
Hospitality House, University of Maryland, Eastern Shore, Princess Anne, Maryland, (410) 651-2200. (This hotel is run by the University's School of Hotel and Restaurant Management and is a tourist bargain.)

16

Princess Anne—Deal Island

Distance: 37.5 miles round trip.
Terrain: Rolling hills and marsh.
Location: Somerset County, Maryland.
Special features: Deal Island Wildlife Management Area, Joshua Thomas Chapel, Wenona.

Heading due west on Route 363 out of Princess Anne, you will have the splendid opportunity of cycling across one of the great marshes of the Chesapeake Bay country. The low and swampy terrain easily gives way to the marsh that stretches to the horizon. Turkey buzzards circle lazily in the sky, and on a crisp fall day the silence of this vast natural area can be awe-inspiring.

One note of caution: The trip across the marsh is strenuous in summer, although it is only little more than 14 miles to the Deal Island Bridge. A summer denizen of the Deal Island Marsh, the greenhead fly can be a painful nuisance. My son Stewart and I foolishly rode across the marsh at the beginning of August when we thought that the greenheads would not be too bad. The flies swarmed all over us, however, and my T-shirt was literally black with them. We were bitten so badly that we were close to tears. The one bright spot of the marsh crossing was that we averaged nearly 18 miles an hour; we were anxious to leave those green-heads behind!

Almost miraculously, the greenheads disappear around the end of September, and from October through April you can enjoy the spectacular beauty of the marsh and be free of insects.

There's history aplenty on this trip as the Deal Island area was one of the first to be settled in this part of the Chesapeake in the late seventeenth century. Deal Island (once known as Devil's Island) was the home of the great evangelical Methodist preacher, Joshua Thomas. This parson of the islands took the half-savage fisher folk of Tangier Island and Deal Island and converted them to Methodism. Deal Islanders were descendants of convicts and indentured servants who had been transported to Maryland Plantation, and they rejected the colder tenets of the Anglican faith. But when Joshua Thomas preached of fire and damnation, using the metaphor and experience of life on the sea, the islanders flocked to the fold.

During the American Revolution, Deal Island was a pirate haven for picaroons who preyed on the naval commerce of the Revolutionary gov-

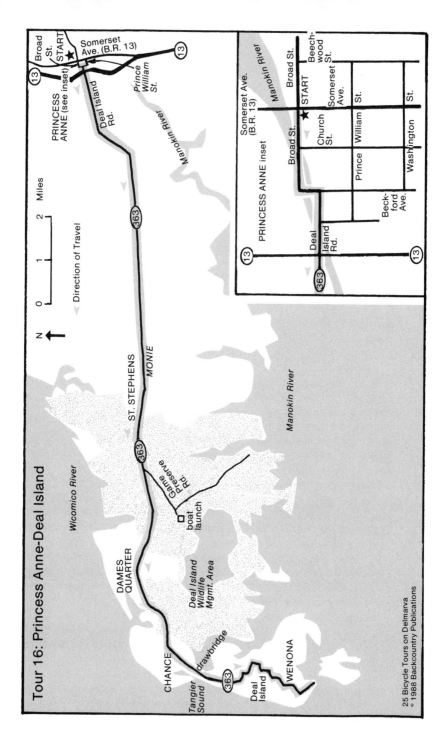

Tour 16: Princess Anne-Deal Island

25 Bicycle Tours on Delmarva
© 1988 Backcountry Publications

ernment and hoped for a Tory victory. Deal Island sits astride Tangier Sound in the Chesapeake and has always been a community of watermen. Although life dependant on the Chesapeake Bay can be tough, Deal Islanders have an earthy sense of humor. A general store in Wenona boasts that the establishment "is not quite at the end of the world, but you can see it from here."

Deal Island is also the home port of the rapidly disappearing fleet of skipjacks. These one-masted sailboats are licensed to pull a dredge across the Chesapeake Bay bottom for oysters. The work is hard and dangerous and fewer skipjacks go out each year during oyster season. Now there are fewer than 30 boats actually working the oyster trade.

Either in port or at sea, the skipjacks are beautiful and serve as a reminder of the nineteenth-century nautical tradition in fishing that has practically vanished along the Atlantic seaboard. When you go to Wenona, take time to look at them and to photograph these proud but declining vessels. They may not be around when you return next.

Directions for the ride

0.0 Our trip begins at the traffic light intersection of Broad Street and Somerset Avenue in Princess Anne. You can easily park your car on any street in the village. **Follow Broad Street west past Tunstall Cottage, the oldest colonial residence in Princess Anne.**

0.2 Turn right on Deal Island Road, which becomes Route 363.

0.3 At the intersection of Route 13 and Route 363, cross Route 13 and head straight on Route 363 for Deal Island. Route 363 crosses farmlands and low forests that gradually recede into the marsh.

8.0 The great Deal Island marsh stretches far to the horizon. The marsh teems with wildlife and is the beginning of the food cycle of the Chesapeake Bay.

> **Side trip:** Just ahead lies the Deal Island Wildlife Management Area. Turn left onto Game Preserve Road. This dirt road ends at a small boat launching site, but you have an uninterrupted view of the marsh far away from the sound of motor traffic. When you return to the highway, turn left on Deal Island Road.

11.3 Enter Dames Quarter, once called Damned Quarter, a farming and fishing village that has a small marina and restaurant. After passing through the hamlets of Monie and St. Stephens, you will think Dames Quarter is a metropolis!

14.0 Come to the village of Chance and the entry to the drawbridge that will take you to Deal Island.

15.1 At the end of the drawbridge enter Deal Island. The Joshua Thomas

The Reverend Joshua Thomas Chapel and graveyard on Deal Island, Maryland.

Teackle Mansion in Princess Anne, Maryland.

Chapel and graveyard dominates Deal Island, and it is easy to tell by the surrounding churches that this is a solid Methodist community. Joshua Thomas preached to the British soldiers on Tangier Island during the War of 1812 and told them that he had been told by God that the British would not rule the Chesapeake Bay. Thomas died in 1853 and is buried in a vault beside the chapel. His epitaph reads: "Come all my friends as you pass by. Behold the place where I do lie. Once as you so was I. Remember you are born to die."

As you cycle across the island, you will notice that the road takes many twists and turns that seem strange until you realize how low the ground is. The road on the island was built on the highest ground to prevent flooding at high tides.

18.7 **Wenona Harbor and boat ramp.** There is a general store here, and you can purchase provisions and eat lunch. Lock up your bike, walk along the wharf, and gaze at the skipjacks or walk out to the shoreline of the island and beachcomb for arrowheads and potsherds.

A note for the return ride

As they say down here on Deal Island, "Honey, you'll have to go back the same way you come in, less you want to swim to Crisfield with that bike."

Bicycle repair services
None on this route.

Lodging
Washington Hotel, Somerset Avenue, Princess Anne, Maryland, (410) 651-2525.

The Lower Chesapeake

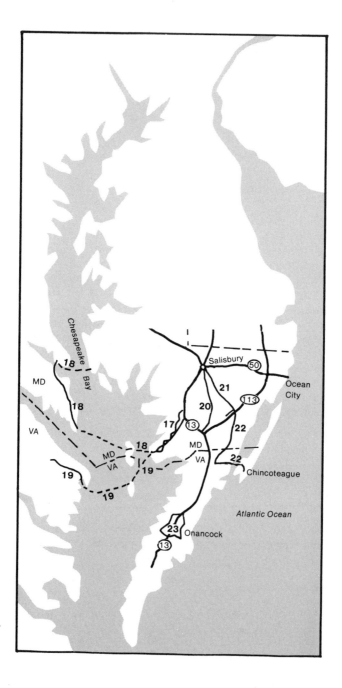

17

Princess Anne—Crisfield Loop

Distance: 45 miles.
Terrain: Flat, occasional marsh and riverfront.
Location: Somerset County, Maryland.
Special features: Princess Anne, Crisfield, Somers Cove Marina, J. Millard Tawes Museum.

The Princess Anne–Crisfield loop is a cycle trip through time that takes bikers through the historic town of Princess Anne and across a region bisected by the Manokin and Annemessex rivers. This area was settled in the seventeenth century by Quakers and political dissenters from the Eastern Shore of Virginia.

During the summer, this route can be exceedingly hot and humid, so pick a cool day for your ride or wait for the weekend weather in autumn. Let two key, regional festivals serve as your guide. On Labor Day weekend Crisfield hosts its annual Hard Crab Derby, a major tourist attraction that features a contest where Chesapeake blue crabs race down a boardway to win prizes for their owners. There are also crab-picking contests, watercraft shows, and country and western music. As civic organizations sell steamed crabs and oyster sandwiches, the Derby is also an adventure in good eating. The 132-slip marina at Somers Cove is a favorite stopover for yachts that are cruising Chesapeake Bay.

In the second weekend of October the village of Princess Anne welcomes over a thousand visitors for its annual Old Princess Anne Days. The town and surrounding area become one large open house, and visitors can see some of the oldest and most elegant plantations and manor houses in the Chesapeake region. Princess Anne celebrates its colonial heritage with militia musters, carriage rides, and a fox hunt.

More information can be obtained on these festivals from the Somerset County Bureau of Tourism, P.O. Box 243, Princess Anne, Maryland 21853, (301) 651-2968.

The Princess Anne–Crisfield loop can be easily done in a day. Also, this loop is good preparation for other bike trips such as tours 16, 18, and 20. Take a weekend and reserve a room at the Washington Hotel in Princess Anne. This antique-filled inn has been in continuous operation since 1745. The inn has a double stairway to the second floor so that women who wore large hoop skirts could pass on the stairs without inconveniencing male guests.

Directions for the ride

0.0   Begin in Princess Anne at the Somerset County Court House at the corner of Somerset Avenue and Prince William Street. There is ample parking space on side streets. Head south on Somerset Avenue.

0.7   Turn right at the Highway Market next to the old warehouse of Kings Creek Cannery onto the beginning of Stewart Neck Road. Enter the Greenwood residential area.

1.1   You will come to Route 13, the major north-south route on the Eastern Shore. Cross Route 13 and continue on Stewart Neck Road.

4.1   Turn right at the stop sign on Revells Neck Road.

5.7   Turn left on Millard Long Road.

8.2   At the stop sign, Millard Long Road becomes River Road. Continue straight. You will travel through some of the beautiful marsh lands of the Annemessex River.

11.3   At the end of River Road, turn right on Charles Cannon Road.

11.8   The road forks here. Keep to the right and continue on Charles Cannon Road. (If you end up on Lovers Lane Road, you've missed the turn!)

13.4   You will reach an intersection and sign for "Marshall's Seafood." Turn left on Burton Road.

15.3   Burton Road leads to Route 413, the Crisfield Highway. Turn right onto Route 413.

16.0   Turn right off of Route 413 at the Texaco Convenience Store and follow Route 667 to Crisfield. Route 667 is also known as the Ward-Crisfield Road.

19.0   At the intersection of Route 413 and Route 667, cross Route 413 and continue on Route 667.

22.0   Enter Crisfield. Route 667 becomes Chesapeake Avenue. At the stop sign, cross Somerset Avenue and continue on Chesapeake Avenue.

22.5   From Chesapeake Avenue, turn left on Maryland Avenue (this is also referred to as Main Street) and head towards the City Municipal Dock. At this point the highway has four lanes. During the summer, Crisfield is a busy town. Watch out for the seafood trucks!

23.3   Crisfield City Dock. You are now in the most important area of town. This is the heart of the maritime commerce of the region and the main street and side streets are lined with restaurants and seafood packing houses. From the dock the view of Tangier Sound is excellent. On a clear day you can see Smith Island, 12 miles due west. The mail and passenger boats for

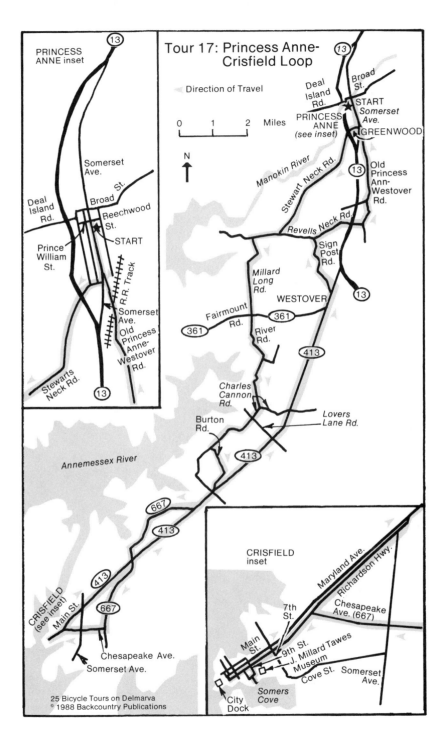

PRINCESS ANNE inset

13

Somerset Ave.

Deal Island Rd.

Broad St.

Beechwood St.

START

Prince William St.

Somerset Ave.

R.R. Track

Old Princess Anne-Westover Rd.

Stewarts Neck Rd.

13

Tour 17: Princess Anne-Crisfield Loop

Direction of Travel

0 1 2 Miles

N

Deal Island Rd.

13

Broad St.

START

Somerset Ave.

PRINCESS ANNE (see inset)

GREENWOOD

Manokin River

Stewart Neck Rd.

13

Old Princess Ann-Westover Rd.

Revells Neck Rd.

Sign Post Rd.

Millard Long Rd.

WESTOVER

13

Fairmount Rd.

361

361

River Rd.

413

Charles Cannon Rd.

Burton Rd.

Lovers Lane Rd.

Annemessex River

413

667

413

413

CRISFIELD (see inset)

Main St.

667

Chesapeake Ave.

Somerset Ave.

CRISFIELD inset

Maryland Ave.

Richardson Hwy.

Chesapeake Ave. (667)

7th St.

Main St.

9th St.

J. Millard Tawes Museum

Cove St.

Somerset Ave.

Somers Cove

City Dock

25 Bicycle Tours on Delmarva
© 1988 Backcountry Publications

Smith Island and Tangier Island depart from here. (See Introduction for ferry schedules.)

A hundred years ago Crisfield prided itself on being the seafood capital of the world. During the heyday of the Chesapeake oyster industry, Crisfield watermen harvested millions of bushels of oysters out of Tangier Sound and shipped them fresh, frozen, or canned to American urban centers and beyond. In 1886, when Chesapeake watermen harvested a record 15 million bushels of oysters from the bay, Crisfield's canned oysters could be purchased in the silver towns of Nevada and in the posh groceries of London's Mayfair. With money to be made and the Chesapeake's mother lode to be looted, Crisfield grew to be a raucus boom town reminiscent of those on the American frontier.

Photo by Orlando V. Wootten

Packing soft shell crabs at the John T. Handy Company in Crisfield, Maryland.

The oyster beds of Tangier Sound have long since been depleted and the pace of Crisfield today is more settled. But the town still retains its hard working salty openness. The oyster and crab packing houses still bustle with activity, especially in late morning when the watermen come to port with their catch.

To sample the maritime flavor of the town, stroll along the docks of Somers Cove Marina. (From the Town Dock, proceed up Maryland Avenue/Main Street to 9th Street and turn right.) Also, visit the J. Millard Tawes Museum with its historical displays of the culture of the Crisfield area.

Near the Town Dock is the popular Ice Cream Gallery. Located in a small alley behind a seafood warehouse, the gallery dispenses large amounts of ice cream to travel-weary cyclists, and the shop's dockside veranda is a favorite with boat watchers and dessert lovers alike.

A note for the return ride

23.3 Head north from the Town Dock out of Crisfield on Richardson Highway, which parallels Maryland Avenue. The two roads eventually merge into Route 413.

37.2 Enter the hamlet of Westover. Turn left at a country church onto Sign Post Road.

39.1 Turn right at the stop sign onto Revells Neck Road. This road will take you past the sprawling Eastern Correctional Facility, one of the largest prisons in Maryland. (Nothing to worry about. Enjoy the scenery.)

40.3 Continue on Revells Neck Road to Route 13. Cross Route 13 and continue straight. A large grain elevator will be on your right.

40.8 At the end of Revells Neck Road, the highway comes to a "T" where there is a stop sign. Turn left. You will be on the old Princess Anne–Westover Road, heading north to Princess Anne.

43.9 Cross the railroad tracks and at the stop sign turn right and continue into Princess Anne on Somerset Avenue.

45.0 Just past the Court House on the left, the Washington Hotel marks the end of your journey.

Bicycle repair services
None on this route.

Lodging
Washington Hotel, 32 Somerset Avenue, Princess Anne, Maryland, (410) 651-2525. Somers Cove Motel, Box 387, Norris Drive, Crisfield, Maryland, (410) 968-1900.

18

Crisfield–Smith Island–Solomons Island–Hoopers Island Loop

Distance: 33 miles by boat, 26 land miles.
Terrain: Flat to rolling countryside.
Location: Somerset County, St. Mary's County, Calvert County, and Dorchester County, Maryland.
Special features: Smith Island, Chesapeake Bay ferries, Point Lookout, Solomons Island.

With the advent of the Chesapeake Bay Ferry Boat Company that operates out of Solomons Island, it is now possible to make a complete land-water loop of the Chesapeake Bay country. I made this loop with my son Stewart in the summer, starting from Crisfield, Maryland, and ending at Fishing Creek Wharf on Hoopers Island in Dorchester County.

On this loop you will see the region as the watermen see it on the bay. As the crow flies, Solomons Island on the western shore is only 15 miles by boat from Hoopers Island on the Eastern Shore. You'll also have an opportunity to visit Smith Island and then ferry across the bay to explore St. Mary's and Calvert counties.

On this loop you will be taking three ferries: *The Island Belle II* out of Crisfield for Smith Island, *The Captain Tyler* out of Smith Island for Point Lookout on the western shore, and the *Mystic* from Solomons Island to Hoopers Island. Figure on ferry fees of $8 per person one way. Also, *The Captain Tyler* charges $2.50 for each bicycle. Please note that you can make this loop only during the May-October tourist season because *The Captain Tyler* and *Mystic* are excursion boats rather than year-round ferries. Ferry captains are an independent lot who tend to interpret their sailing schedules loosely, so it always pays to check with the ferry operators well in advance.

The Captain Tyler
Allen Tyler, Captain
Runs Memorial Day through September 30
Ewell, Smith Island, to Point Lookout
Daily: 2:00 P.M.
(301) 425-2771

The Island Belle II
(see Introduction for ferry schedule)

Mystic
Cynthia Rigg, Captain
Runs Memorial Day through October
Solomons Island to Hoopers Island
Wednesday, Saturday, and Sunday only
Leaves Solomons Island for Hoopers Island at 9:00 A.M.
Reservations requested
(301) 326-3379

Directions for the ride

0.0   Town Dock at Crisfield. If you are being dropped off by car in Crisfield for this loop, plan to be picked up the next day around 11:00 A.M. at the public landing wharf at Fishing Creek on Hoopers Island in Dorchester County. I do not recommend closing the loop by continuing from Hoopers Island to Crisfield. It is simply too hot, too long, and too physically problematic. Heed the words of one who has done it!

The Town Dock at Crisfield is always abuzz with activity in the late morning. The 50-passenger mail boat, *Island Belle II,* is being loaded with groceries and other necessities, and you may find your bike lashed on deck to an old refrigerator. The boat is often crammed to the gills with freight boxes, groceries, and passengers. Captain Otis Tyler oversees the loading of *Island Belle II* and pays for all the provisions from a huge cash roll. (That's the way business is done out on the bay! Watermen don't have much use for checks and credit cards, though they'll trust your word.) **The *Island Belle II* leaves the dock promptly at 12:30 P.M. for Smith Island. On a "slick calm" day the ferry ride to the island takes 40 minutes.**

When the boat arrives at Ewell on Smith Island, check at the dock to learn where *The Captain Tyler* is moored. The boat originates from Point Lookout, and usually departs at 2:00 P.M. with a boat load of holiday excursionists from the western shore. You will have about a 40-minute wait before you depart for Point Lookout, which is ample time to stretch your legs with a ride around Smith Island.

Smith Islanders are almost entirely of British ancestry, and their dialect may be a bit hard to understand. Everyone here depends on the Chesapeake Bay for his or her livelihood, and you will see plenty of boat traffic at the Ewell harbor. Named for Captain John Smith who sailed the Chesapeake in 1608, Smith Island has a population of about 750—mostly stout, God-fearing Methodists to the man. The Ewell Methodist Church is the central part of island life. There are no bars or taverns on this island.

Despite the difficulties of wresting a living from the Chesapeake Bay, islanders resist the attractions of the mainland economy. The only conces-

Tour 18: Crisfield-Smith Island-Solomons Island-Hoopers Island Loop

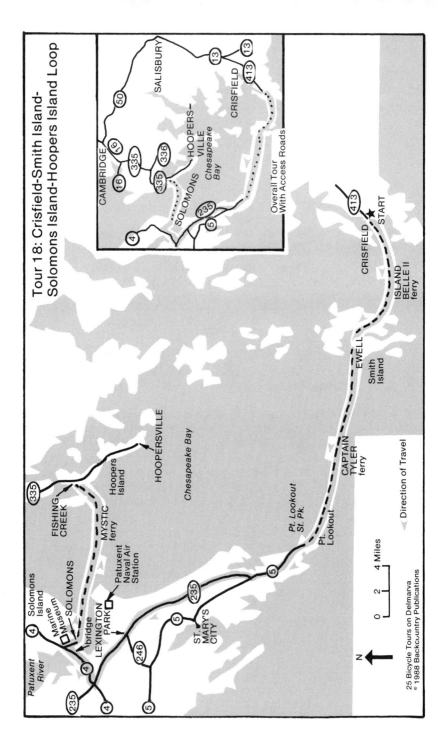

SALISBURY

CAMBRIDGE

HOOPERS-VILLE

CRISFIELD

Chesapeake Bay

SOLOMONS

Overall Tour With Access Roads

CRISFIELD

START

ISLAND BELLE II ferry

EWELL

Smith Island

CAPTAIN TYLER ferry

Pt. Lookout St. Pk.

Pt. Lookout

Chesapeake Bay

HOOPERSVILLE

Hoopers Island

FISHING CREEK

MYSTIC ferry

Patuxent Naval Air Station

SOLOMONS

LEXINGTON PARK

ST. MARY'S CITY

Solomons Island

Marine Museum

bridge

Patuxent River

N

0   2   4 Miles

25 Bicycle Tours on Delmarva
© 1988 Backcountry Publications

Direction of Travel

sion they make is to send their children to high school every day in Crisfield on a high speed school boat.

At 2:00 P.M. *The Captain Tyler* whistles its impending departure, and you better scramble aboard quickly for the two-hour ride to Point Lookout on the western shore. The boat will dock at Point Lookout State Park usually between 3:30 and 4:00 P.M. The one drawback to the timing of this ride is that you will have to bicycle through busy Lexington Park, Maryland, at the height of the rush hour.

0.0   **Point Lookout State Park.** A lovely state park that offers vistas of the bay, camping, and picnic facilities, Point Lookout State Park was tailor-made for bikers on a budget. There is a camp store at the marina and ample tent sites for weary cyclists who do not wish to push onto Solomons Island in the late afternoon.

During the Civil War, this area was the site of the notorious Point Lookout Confederate Prisoner of War Camp. Many rebel prisoners of war perished here of malnutrition and the harsh environment. Point Lookout Camp was known as the Andersonville of the North. There is a Confederate cemetery and monument just outside the park.

From the wharf at Point Lookout State Park, turn left out of the boat ramp/parking lot.

1.9   Turn left onto Route 5.

6.0   Turn right on Route 235.

Side Trip: If you wish to go to Historic St. Mary's City, continue north on Route 5. Three and a half centuries ago, 140 English settlers came here to begin the Maryland colony for Lord Baltimore. Today the state maintains an 850-acre outdoor museum dedicated to the early seventeenth-century origins of the state. A replica of the *Dove,* one of the sailing vessels that carried settlers from England to the Chesapeake in the seventeenth century, is moored here. The park, museum, and visitors center is open daily to the public from 10:00 A.M. to 5:00 P.M. For further information, write to Historic St. Mary's City, P.O. Box 39, St. Mary's City, Maryland.

16.0   **Patuxent Naval Air Station.** Traffic in the vicinity of this sprawling military base can be quite busy. You will pass the base on your right. Keep well to the right on this highway.

18.2   **Lexington Park.** Formerly a sleepy crossroads village, Lexington Park now caters to the needs of the large military base. There are plenty of markets and convenience stores here. The rush-hour traffic seems odd when you consider that you are still in a rural area far removed from Washington and Annapolis. Everyone in Lexington Park seems to work at the base, and they are anxious to get home at quitting time. At the junction of Route 246 and Route 235, continue on Route 235.

22.8   Turn right on Route 4 north.

25.0   **Patuxent River Bridge.** Because of the rush-hour traffic, I found crossing the bridge an ordeal. The bridge is steep and requires hard pedaling. From the crest of the bridge on a clear day you can see Hoopers Island, so be advised that the bridge is not for the faint-hearted. Also, after the crest of the bridge, resist the urge to go hell-for-leather downhill. There are some nasty ruts in the asphalt at the bottom of the bridge, so be careful.

26.5   **Enter Solomons Island,** which is well worth the aggravation of the Patuxent River Bridge. Formerly a large fishing and oystering community, Solomons Island is now the sailing mecca of Maryland and the unofficial headquarters of the Chesapeake yachtsman. The community is named for Isaac Solomon, a Civil War-era oyster broker who operated a seafood cannery here. On the Patuxent side of the island is one of the great harbors of the East Coast. The harbor is two miles wide and in places over 100 feet deep. Small wonder that Solomons is the darling port of the yachting crowd.

   Although Solomons Island receives a heavy influx of tourists in summer, it does not appeal to the beach crowd. Both visitors and residents alike are affluent and well-travelled. Although there are many good restaurants and interesting shops, you will find little resort glitz here.

The mailboat *Island Belle II* at the Crisfield dock.

The pride of Solomons Island is the Calvert Marine Museum that is located at the entrance to Solomons Island on your left. It contains the famous Drum Point Light House and the J.C. Lore Oyster House, a completely restored turn-of-the-century seafood packing house. The museum has received national recognition as a maritime educational center that attracts as many as 50,000 visitors a year. It is a must stop for anyone who wants to learn about prehistoric fossils, explore a tidal marsh, or cruise on a Chesapeake work boat.

A note for the return trip

Remember that the *Mystic* runs only on Wednesdays, Saturdays, and Sundays in season. The night before your departure, call Captain Rigg to assure your berth on the ferry. Although the *Mystic* is moored nine miles by road out of town at Drum Point, the boat has but a short distance to go across the harbor to pick up you and your bike at the Lore Oyster Packing House. If you are elsewhere on Solomons Island, Captain Rigg can be paged on ship-to-shore radio and you can arrange a pick up point at the harbor. Travel on the *Mystic* is definitely a luxury experience. You will not regret it.

The *Mystic* departs Solomons Island at 9:00 A.M. Depending on the weather, expect to arrive at Hoopers Island between 10:30 and 11:00.A.M. (For a description of Hoopers Island, see Tour 11.) As you approach Hoopers Island, you will see hundreds of small buoys that mark the crab pots of the islanders.

If you require land transportation to Cambridge or elsewhere in the vicinity, you can arrange to be met by van by calling Glyndon Loof, Casual Tours, Box 800, Cambridge, Maryland 21613, (301) 228-9139.

Bicycle repair services

Mike's Bikes, 447-C, Great Mills Road, Lexington Park, Maryland, (301) 863-7887.

Lodging

Island Manor Motel, 1 Main Street, Solomons, Maryland, (410) 326-3700.

19

Crisfield—Tangier Island—Reedville, Virginia

Distance: 34 miles by boat, 29 land miles.
Terrain: Chesapeake Bay, rolling countryside.
Location: Somerset County, Maryland, and Northumberland County, Virginia.
Special features: Ferry crossing of Chesapeake Bay, Tangier Island, Northern Neck of Virginia, side trip to Williamsburg.

This is the second tour that combines cycling with a boat excursion across the Chesapeake Bay. The advent of tourism has sparked a salutary development in the bay country—the renewal of ferry excursions on the Chesapeake. It is now possible to cross the bay from either Onancock, Virginia, or Crisfield, Maryland, via Tangier Island and arrive at the western shore of the Chesapeake in Virginia. However, service is seasonal so plan this tour between Memorial Day and Labor Day. Sometimes the ferry continues into the fall while the weather is good, but it is chancy at best after September 15.

This combined land and water route is excellent for cyclists who have never before seen the Chesapeake Bay in all of its summer splendor. Ospreys nest on buoy lights, and at times swarms of dolphins and bluefish slice through the water. Out in the bay's main channel, ocean-going vessels ply the main route from Norfolk to Baltimore.

Tangier Island remains an intriguing Methodist stronghold of sturdy seafaring families whose language and way of life has hardly changed over the centuries. Men harvest blue crabs and tithe weekly to their church.

The Northern Neck District of Virginia is one of the most isolated and rural regions of the state. Although Northumberland County is less than 70 miles from Richmond, it still retains a remoteness and provinciality of the South as it was in the 1930s. This is one of the few areas that has not been contaminated by the neon, fast-food culture that has disrupted many towns and villages on the Chesapeake.

This tour opens extended possibilities for travel in Virginia as colonial Williamsburg, Richmond, and Washington are easily accessible to seasoned bikers.

Directions for the ride

0.0   Town Dock, Crisfield. Our trip begins in Crisfield, Maryland. The best strategy is to park your car in the Somers Cove Marina parking lot or on one of the side streets, if you plan to return via the same route. The boat for Tangier Island, *The Steven Thomas,* leaves the wharf at 10th Street every day at 12:30 P.M. The crew of *The Steven Thomas* is experienced in dealing with cyclists, and your bicycle will be stowed safely and securely. The one-way fare to Tangier Island is $8.00 and worth every penny as you go bounding across the waves of the Chesapeake. It is about 16 nautical miles from Crisfield to Tangier Island.

16.0   Tangier Island. Tangier is a self-sufficient island of crabbers and fishermen. It has a small airstrip, and its school offers public education from the first through the twelfth grade. The school population of 115 makes it one of the smallest in the state, but education is held in high esteem among the 750 islanders, and many graduates of the Island School have gone on to make their mark in Virginia society. Tangier is a conservative, religious Methodist community, and there are no bars or cocktail lounges on the island.

Tangier Island is a delight for both the novice and experienced cyclist. There are no cars on the island, and the only traffic consists of other bikes and a small fleet of golf carts used for sightseeing. **The main path consists of a 2.5-mile loop around the island past the neatly kept and prosperous homes of watermen. Tangier can be easily explored in a few hours.**

As you cycle through Tangier, notice one of the intriguing features of the island – the individual cemeteries in the front yards of many homes. As the water table is quite high, the graves are covered with heavy cement slabs to prevent tidal water pressure from forcing burial vaults to the surface.

Tangier is well known for its home-cooked seafood dinners, and at Hilda Crockett's Chesapeake House the family-style dinners are "all you can eat." Many tourists are overwhelmed by the abundant meals. After lunch there is time to visit one of the numerous soft crab shanties and watch watermen separate and box soft crabs (crabs that have lost their shell and can be eaten whole) for market.

At 4:00 P.M. the excursion boat *Chesapeake Breeze* departs Tangier Island for Reedville, Virginia. After a crew member stows your bike, the purser will sell you a one-way ticket for $9.00. The trip to Reedville is 18 nautical miles.

34.0   Enter the port of Reedville. As you enter Reedville, you will see numerous estates and fine homes near the water's edge. Flocks of ducks and sea gulls and boats bobbing gently in the water make Reedville a charming Chesapeake scene. Occasionally, the smell of a nearby fish processing plant is a bit disturbing, however. Reedville is the home port of the

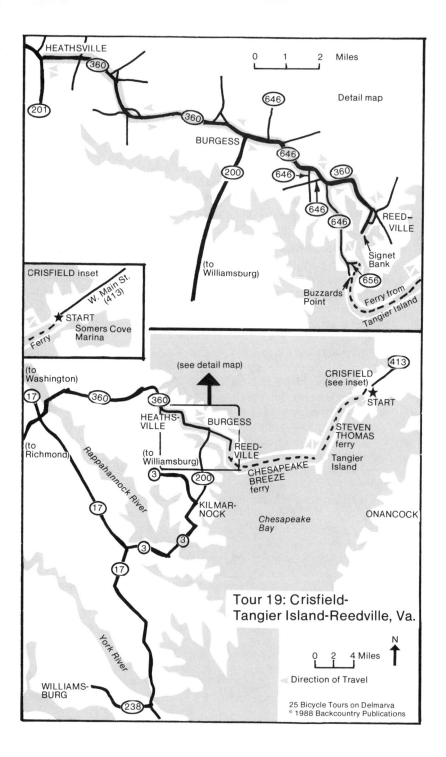

HEATHSVILLE

360

201

646

Detail map

0   1   2   Miles

360

BURGESS

646

200

646   646   360

646

646

REED-
VILLE

Signet
Bank

656

Buzzards
Point

(to
Williamsburg)

Ferry from

Tangier Island

CRISFIELD inset

W. Main St.
(413)

START
Somers Cove
Marina

Ferry

(to Washington)

17

360

360

(see detail map)

CRISFIELD
(see inset)

413

START

(to
Richmond)

HEATHS-
VILLE

BURGESS

REED-
VILLE

STEVEN
THOMAS
ferry

Rappahannock River

(to Williamsburg)

3

200

CHESAPEAKE
BREEZE
ferry

Tangier
Island

17

KILMAR-
NOCK

Chesapeake
Bay

ONANCOCK

3

3

17

Tour 19: Crisfield-
Tangier Island-Reedville, Va.

York River

N

0   2   4 Miles

WILLIAMS-
BURG

238

Direction of Travel

25 Bicycle Tours on Delmarva
© 1988 Backcountry Publications

Chesapeake Bay menhaden fleet. Most of the fish caught by this fleet are processed for cat food. Some of it is also used for making fertilizer. **The Chesapeake Breeze docks at Buzzard's Point, and here you will find a picnic area with an excellent waterfront view. From Buzzard's Point the land portion of our trip begins.**

0.0 Buzzards Point. Take Route 656 one-half mile to Route 646. Turn right on Route 646.

1.9 Turn right on Route 360 to Reedville.

4.0 **Enter Reedville.** A small Victorian town, Reedville in the past was known as the home of Chesapeake Bay pilots and boat captains. Many were quite prosperous and built solid, imposing homes that can be seen at considerable distances out on the bay. The homes have large porches and backyards that slope toward deep creeks. In Reedville nearly everyone has a boat moored at a pier jutting out from the backyard.

5.0 **The highway dead-ends at a seafood packing house and the Signet Bank.** Many residents go out on the water early in the morning so the streets of this town are usually deserted by sunset. People lead a quiet life in Northumberland County. **At the Signet Bank turn around and head north on Route 360.**

11.2 Enter the village of Burgess.
Side Trip: From Burgess you can make a 90-mile overnight side trip to Williamsburg. To go to Williamsburg, turn left on Route 200, then pick up Route 3 at Kilmarnock. Proceed to the Rappahannock River Bridge. From the bridge continue south on Route 3 to Route 17. Route 17 is a four-lane highway that should be used with caution. It will take you to Route 238, the Colonial Parkway, to Williamsburg.

19.6 **Continuing on Route 360, enter Heathsville, the county seat of Northumberland County.** Heathsville is a quiet antebellum village that still remembers its Confederate dead. Walk around the courthouse grounds and pay special attention to the ruined building behind the courthouse that was once the lawyers row and center of town business life. Heathsville is so quiet that it is hard to believe that we are nearly within automobile commuting distance of Richmond. But then, that is life on the farm and in the villages of the Northern Neck of Virginia—quiet, very quiet.

A note for the return ride

Retrace your steps south on Route 360 to Reedville. Two miles out of Reedville is the Bay Motel, the area's ONLY motel. Spend the night here if you wish to take the *Chesapeake Breeze* back to Tangier Island. The boat departs Buzzard's Point at 10:00 A.M. The area's ONLY restaurant, the Tripp-A-Lee Restaurant, is one mile from the Bay Motel and opens for breakfast at 5:00 A.M. The restaurant is two miles from Buzzard's Point and it is an easy jaunt through cornfield-lined highway to the boat.

Bicycle repair services
None on this route.

Lodging
Chesapeake House, (Open April 15–October 15), Tangier Island, Maryland, (804) 891-2331.

Bay Motel, Route 360, Reedville, Virginia, (804) 453-5171.

20

Salisbury—Pocomoke City

Distance: 35 miles one way.
Terrain: Flat to gently rolling.
Location: Wicomico County and Worcester County, Maryland.
Special features: Pocomoke Forest, Nassawango Iron Furnace, Pocomoke City.

A cycle trip to Pocomoke City from Salisbury is a refreshing excursion. The route takes you through the heart of the Pocomoke State Forest on the periphery of the wild cypress swamps of the Pocomoke River. Even in the midst of an Eastern Shore summer, most of the route is cool — protected by a beautiful canopy of forest that bathes the highway in shadows. Those of you who have cycled across the open farm lands of the upper Chesapeake in summer will greatly appreciate this route.

This route is not a loop, so unless you want to retrace the route on your bike, you will need to arrange transportation back to the starting point when you arrive in Pocomoke City. (If you wish, you can bike 27.5 miles up Route 13 north to Salisbury. The road, though busy, has a large, safe shoulder.)

The forests and swamps of the Pocomoke River have their own illustrious past. Rich in game, they were the haunt of the Nanticoke and Wicomico Indians. Later in the antebellum era, they served as a hideaway for runaway slaves. The Pocomoke Swamp sustains many cypress trees and over the centuries has supported local lumber industries. Bog iron mined from the swamp was smelted into pig iron at the Nassawango Iron Furnace in the heart of the Pocomoke Forest.

Since colonial times, the Pocomoke River has been an important artery of commerce. It is an exceptionally deep river, and Chesapeake vessels carrying petroleum and fertilizer ply its waters.

On this route you will have an excellent chance to see some of the wildlife of the Eastern Shore. The Pocomoke Forest is full of deer, and the rich bird life makes it a bird watcher's delight.

Directions for the ride

0.0 Start at the intersection of College Avenue and Camden Avenue at Salisbury State College. Follow College Avenue east to Route 13.

0.3 Cross Route 13 and head east on College Avenue.

0.5   Turn right on South Division Street.

1.8   Veer left onto Coulbourne Mill Road off South Division Street.

3.1   Turn right on Union Church Road. This will take you past Deer Harbor, an affluent Salisbury subdivision.

4.7   Turn right onto Old Pocomoke Road. This will take you down through the Pocomoke Forest and into Worcester County. There are no stores or service stations along this route for the next 30 miles.

10.7   At the intersection of Old Pocomoke Road and Old Furnace Road, turn left on Old Furnace Road, which will take you through a portion of the Pocomoke Swamp. Although there has been a significant amount of logging in this area, the forest and swamp here are still wild and intriguing.
    Alternate route: If you wish to turn this route into a loop back to Salisbury, continue on Old Furnace Road to Route 12/Snow Hill Road. At the intersection of Old Furnace Road and Route 12 you have two options. You can turn left to Salisbury and finish the loop or else turn right and proceed into Snow Hill.

16.7   Nassawango Iron Furnace. Between 1832 and 1847 the Nassawango Iron Furnace supported a flourishing community of miners, sawyers, colliers, moulders, and laborers who were engaged in mining low grade bog iron from the Pocomoke Forest and Swamp for the large Nassawango iron smelter. The furnace itself was 35 feet high with hot blast tubes built into the top. During its operation, the furnace was loaded with layers of charcoal, bog iron, and oyster shells until it was filled. When heated to moulten level, pure iron was let out at the casting hearth and cooled into two-foot-long bars of pig iron. Boats were then loaded with the iron and floated down the nearby Nassawango Creek and thence down the Pocomoke River to the Chesapeake Bay, Baltimore, and beyond. The furnace ceased operation in 1847 when new types of furnaces using better quality iron ore forced the little "Furnace Town" out of business.
    Today you can still see the Nassawango Iron Furnace and walk over the grounds of what was once a 5,000-acre smelting and mining operation. A number of nineteenth-century dwellings have been moved to the grounds, and the area is now a public park and museum with guided tours and an operational blacksmith shop. Nassawango Iron Furnace is listed in the National Register of Historic Places and is open April through October. For information, telephone (301) 632-2032.

22.7   Retrace your route, returning to the intersection of Old Furnace Road and Old Pocomoke Road. Turn left on Old Pocomoke Road. **Caution:** Old Pocomoke Road suffers from several name changes, which is at times confusing. But it is the only due south road in the area, so stay on it. At this point Old Pocomoke Road becomes Whiteburg Road.

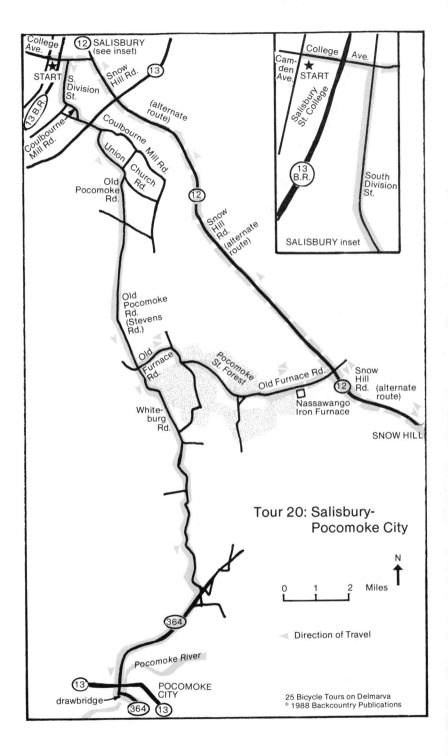

College Ave.

(12) SALISBURY
(see inset)

START

Snow Hill Rd.

(13)

S. Division St.

13 B.R.

(alternate route)

Coulbourne Mill Rd.

Coulbourne Mill Rd.

Union

Church Rd.

Old Pocomoke Rd.

(12)

Snow Hill Rd. (alternate route)

Old Pocomoke Rd. (Stevens Rd.)

Old Furnace Rd.

Pocomoke St. Forest

Old Furnace Rd.

Snow Hill Rd. (alternate route)

(12)

Nassawango Iron Furnace

Whiteburg Rd.

SNOW HILL

Tour 20: Salisbury-Pocomoke City

N

0   1   2   Miles

(364)

Direction of Travel

(13)

drawbridge

Pocomoke River

POCOMOKE CITY

(364) (13)

25 Bicycle Tours on Delmarva
© 1988 Backcountry Publications

SALISBURY inset

College Ave.

Camden Ave.

★ START

Salisbury St. College

13 B.R.

South Division St.

SALISBURY inset

Nassawango Iron Furnace.

30.5   At the end of Old Pocomoke Road/Whiteburg Road, turn right on Route 364.

33.4   Dividing Creek Market and Country Store.

34.8   There is a traffic light at the intersection of Route 364 and Route 13. Cross Route 13 and follow Route 364 to the left, crossing the Pocomoke River drawbridge.

35.2   Enter Pocomoke City. An old river town that is located about ten miles from the mouth of the river, Pocomoke City retains its regional flavor and heritage. Though the steamboats that once gave the town its prosperity as a commercial and agricultural entrepot are long gone, Pocomoke is still a neat and tidy town of small shops, churches, and restaurants. Explore the town's river walk that runs in an east-west direction immediately after the drawbridge.

There are fast food restaurants and motels conveniently located on nearby Route 13, which runs parallel to the town's main thoroughfare. Also, Pocomoke City is an excellent launching site for bike trips either to Snow Hill or Virginia's Eastern Shore.

Bicycle repair services
Salisbury Schwinn Cyclery, 1404 South Salisbury Boulevard, Salisbury, Maryland, (410) 546-4747.

Lodging
Days Inn, Route 13, Pocomoke City, Maryland, (410) 957-3000.

21

Salisbury—Snow Hill

Distance: 18 miles one way.
Terrain: Flat to rolling countryside.
Location: Wicomico County, and Worcester County, Maryland.
Special features: Snow Hill, Shad Landing State Park.

The trip to Snow Hill is a perfect cycle outing for those who wish to combine a day of biking with a picnic and a self-guided exploration of a Victorian town and a very popular state park. Also, the bike ride to Snow Hill offers a number of possibilities for the experienced cyclist. You can push onto Chincoteague (see Tour 22) or take the loop down to Iron Furnace and either Pocomoke City or Princess Anne (see Tour 20 and Tour 17).

Chartered in 1686, Snow Hill is the county seat of Worcester County and an important regional center. Though the town may give the first time visitor the impression that this is just another sleepy Eastern Shore town, nothing could be farther from the truth. Snow Hill is an important legal center (all the legal matters of Ocean City must be taken care of here) and a major agricultural town. It is also the gateway for tourism in Worcester County. Snow Hill, for example, is well known as a place for canoeing, picnicking, hiking, bird watching, and nature walks.

The local architecture of Snow Hill is most impressive, and the colonial and nineteenth-century examples are exceptional. Snow Hill's great gem is All Hallows Episcopal Church, which was established in 1692; the present structure was built in 1756. In those days, the cost of construction was measured in pounds of tobacco, and All Hallows cost 80,000 pounds of the "royal weed." You can cycle through the historic district and see many of Snow Hill's fine homes from curb side. Unlike many other areas, every day people from all walks of life continue to live and raise families in these exceptionally fine colonial and Victorian homes. The town has not yet been gentrified by wealthy outsiders from the western shore.

In the seventeenth century, Snow Hill was a royal port with direct access to London. The Pocomoke River with its deep water easily accommodated colonial ocean-going commerce, and Snow Hill carried on a lively trade with London. After the Revolution, Snow Hill was an important ship-building center and steamboat landing. Originally part of Somerset

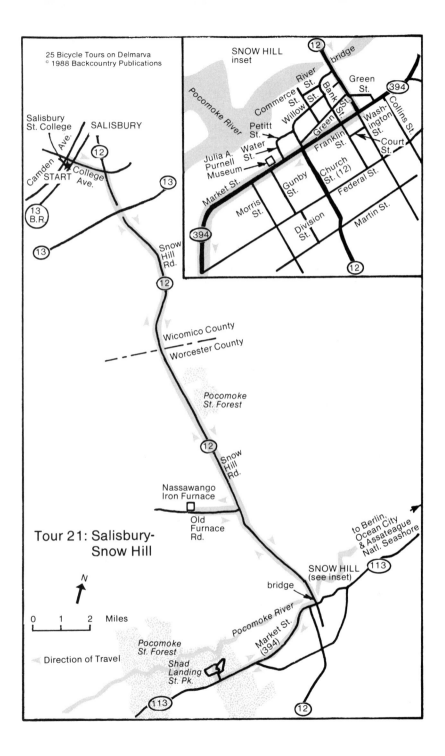

25 Bicycle Tours on Delmarva
© 1988 Backcountry Publications

Salisbury
St. College

SALISBURY

Camden
Ave.

College
Ave.

START

12

13
B.R.

13

13

Snow
Hill
Rd.

12

Wicomico County

Worcester County

Pocomoke
St. Forest

12

Snow
Hill
Rd.

Nassawango
Iron Furnace

Old
Furnace
Rd.

Tour 21: Salisbury-
Snow Hill

N

0   1   2   Miles

Direction of Travel

Pocomoke
St. Forest

Shad
Landing
St. Pk.

113

Pocomoke River

Market St.
(394)

SNOW HILL
(see inset)

bridge

to Berlin,
Ocean City
& Assateague
Natl. Seashore

113

12

SNOW HILL
inset

12

bridge

Pocomoke River

Commerce
St.

River
St.

Willow
St.

Bank St.

Green
St.

394

Washington
St.

Collins St.

Petitt
St.

Green
St.

Franklin
St.

Court
St.

Julia A.
Purnell
Museum

Water
St.

Market St.

Gunby
St.

Church
St. (12)

Federal St.

Morris
St.

Division
St.

Martin St.

394

12

County, Snow Hill became the administrative center of Worcester County when it was formed in 1754.

You will enjoy the quiet, brick-sidewalked and tree-lined streets of Snow Hill. Also, the town has an excellent Victorian restaurant, the Snow Hill Inn, which has some of the finest Eastern Shore cooking to be found in the region. If you stay overnight at the inn, at least you will be assured of a sitting at the evening meal, which is always by reservation only.

You can get a brochure at the Tourist Office in the nearby Court House that describes a walking tour of the town. I would like to recommend the following houses that are well worth seeing on your cycle trip to Snow Hill:

1. Chanceford. This large Federal-period house on 209 Federal Street was built in 1792 supposedly for Robert Morris, the "financier of the American Revolution." The floors and woodwork are original, and the house has seven working fireplaces.

2. The Teagle-Townsend House on 208 W. Federal Street was built around 1814. A great chimney dominates the south end of the house.

While I am not an architectural expert, I have chosen these two houses to whet your appetite to explore Federal Street in Snow Hill and to explore the other avenues in this historically rich town. By all means, get the walking tour brochure and embark on an adventure in history!

Afterwards, when you have seen the town and lunched at the Snow Hill Inn, it will be time to press on to Shad Landing State Park. Locals call it Shad Landing, but its official name is the Shad Landing Area of Pocomoke River State Park. Shad Landing is one of two separate areas of the state park. Also, what is especially appealing about this cycle route is that it provides you with opportunities to take either guided canoe trips or self-directed trips through the great Pocomoke Swamp.

This is an easy route; the highway is flat and the way from Salisbury to Snow Hill is well marked, which makes it an excellent tour for the novice cyclist who may be worried about his/her physical ability to complete the tour.

This tour is one way, so you should arrange to be met by car or van in Snow Hill if you do not choose to push on to other destinations.

Directions for the ride

0.0   The trip begins in Salisbury at the intersection of College Avenue and Camden Avenue at the corner of Salisbury State College. As in tours 13, 15, and 20, we begin here because it is convenient for parking and the outward route offers minimum automobile traffic. Turn right on College Avenue.

1.42   Turn right on Route 12/Snow Hill Road. The Holly Center, an institution for developmentally disabled youth, will be on your right.

The Worcester County Courthouse in Snow Hill, Maryland.

Photo by Orlando V. Wootten

7.3   **Worcester County line.** The road widens here and you will have a much better shoulder to ride on than you did coming out of Salisbury.

13.9   **Nassawango Iron Furnace Road.** If you wish, you can turn right here to go to the Furnace Town Museum and Park, the site of a great bog iron furnace for smelting iron ore in the nineteenth century (see Tour 20).

17.9   **Pocomoke River Bridge. Enter Snow Hill.** Adjacent to this old drawbridge is the Pocomoke River Canoe Company, which rents canoes for people who wish to explore the Pocomoke River and its environs. Once out on the river you will enter the same kind of habitat that colonial settlers saw, and your chances of spotting osprey, blue heron, egrets, and other wildlife are excellent. The boats come equipped with life vests. The Pocomoke River Canoe Company also conducts group tours of the Pocomoke Swamp, a beautiful primitive tract of white oak, bald cypress, and picturesque water routes. (The Canoe Company is open Memorial Day–Labor Day, Barry Laws, Proprietor, (301) 632-3971.)

18.0   **Turn right on Market Street in Snow Hill. This will put you in the center of town. Follow Market Street to the Julia Purnell Museum** (208 W. Market Street), which houses an interesting collection of nineteenth-century memorabilia. Here you will be able to see Victorian needlework, old farm tools, spinning wheels, kitchen equipment, antique toys, and Indian artifacts. The museum is open weekdays 9:00 A.M. to 5:00 P.M.; weekends 1:00 to 5:00 P.M. (301) 632-0515.

18.2   **If you wish to continue on to Shad Landing State Park, continue on Market Street out of Snow Hill. Market Street becomes Route 394, which takes you to Route 113.**

21.2   **Turn right into Shad Landing State Park.** This park takes its name from former days when the area was popular with shad fishermen as a harbor and landing on the Pocomoke River. In addition to a large picnic area along the river, the park has a campground. You also can rent canoes and motor boats and travel through a small well-marked portion of the Pocomoke Swamp. In the late afternoon it is pleasant to ride along the park road down to the river wharf and watch pleasure boats coming up from the Chesapeake moor for the night. Also, if you camp at Shad Landing, you are permitted to use the park swimming pool.

A note for the return ride

Simply retrace your route back to Snow Hill. If you wish a lengthier trip, you can proceed up Route 113, which will take you to Berlin and routes to Assateague National Seashore and Ocean City (see Tour 25).

Bicycle repair services

Salisbury Schwinn Cyclery, 1404 South Salisbury Boulevard (Route 13), Salisbury, Maryland, (410) 546-4747.

Lodging

Snow Hill Inn, 104 E. Market Street, Snow Hill, Maryland, (410) 632-2102.

22

Snow Hill, Maryland—Chincoteague, Virginia

Distance: 47 miles one way.
Terrain: Flat to rolling countryside.
Location: Worcester County, Maryland, and Accomack County, Virginia.
Special features: Chincoteague Island, Chincoteague National Wildlife Refuge.

This trip should be considered in conjunction with Tour 20 and Tour 21. These three tours make an excellent weekend of cross-country cycling in any season and offer a combination of small towns, historic centers, and scenic natural environments.

There is a certain enchantment about Chincoteague. Perhaps it stems from the romantic tales of lost pirate treasure and herds of wild horses that have roamed on the island since the sixteenth century. Perhaps it is the golden brown expanses of marsh and wild seashore that form a rare setting in the mid-Atlantic region.

Chincoteague lies just beyond Chincoteague Channel, a large shallow body of water traversed by a narrow strip of highway. Although settlers from the Jamestown colony of Virginia came here over three centuries ago, the town remained an isolated fishing village on a remote island until the state connected it to the mainland with a causeway in 1922.

By any resort standard, Chincoteague Island is small. Its population of 3,555 is set in its ways, and islanders are in no hurry to emulate towns to the north like Cape May and Ocean City. The town is more or less a simple village of narrow crisscrossing streets, and the flavor of local life is more of New England than of the South. The houses are simple white clapboard, and there are few bars and resort nightspots. On a summer night in Chincoteague, the most exciting spots in town are the local ice-cream parlors.

Chincoteague is famous for its salty oysters and seafood, and the town is still the home port of a large commercial fishing fleet. Lately Chincoteague has also become known as the home port for charter boats engaged in shark fishing. This dangerous sport has become popular with affluent tourists, and on the day I cycled to Chincoteague, I spotted several large sharks hanging as trophies near one of the boat wharves.

The Chincoteague Wildlife Refuge is just a short ride out of town. Created in 1943, the refuge has over 9,000 acres of land, and within that area are some of the finest stretches of unbroken primal beach, rolling dunes, marshes, and freshwater ponds. The chief citizens of the island are the Chincoteague wild ponies. Though they love to cadge snacks from sympathetic tourists and appear docile, they are wild animals; they can bite and kick, so respect them. In July the Chincoteague Fire Department stages its annual Pony Swim and Penning. To preserve the ecological balance of the herd, ponies are culled and sold at auction. This popular event attracts thousands of tourists and is fun to see and photograph.

If you want to experience the island as the locals do, come to Chincoteague in the fall after the tourists have gone. There is no hectic rush to get to the beach, and traffic on the causeway to the island is less bothersome.

The Indians called the island Gingoteague, the beautiful land across the water. When you come to Chincoteague you will see that the Indians were right.

Directions for the ride

0.0   **The trip begins at the old drawbridge on Route 12, just as you enter Snow Hill from Salisbury.** You will find ample parking for your car on the side streets around the new county library and municipal building (see the map of Snow Hill: Tour 21).

0.2   **Turn right on Market Street.**

0.3   **Turn left on Church Street/Route 12 and follow the signs for Girdletree and Stockton.**

1.8   **Intersection and stop sign at Route 113. Cross Route 113 and continue on Route 12.**

6.1   **Enter the village of Girdletree.** There is a country market that sells cold drinks and snacks.

9.1   **Reach the village of Stockton.** In this area there is a kosher poultry plant and occasionally tourists are surprised to see orthodox Jewish butchers from New York City in this remote rural hamlet.

9.6   **Flemings Grocery and intersection of Route 366. Continue straight, south on Route 12.**

13.0 **Virginia State line. Route 12 becomes Route 679. Continue south on Route 679.** The land becomes more rolling now and distances between villages and towns are longer.

16.8 **Enter Horntown, Virginia.**

21.0 **At the intersection of Route 679 and Route 175, turn left on Route 175.** Coffins Market is a good place to stop for a lunch of homemade sandwiches.

Wild ponies at Chincoteague.

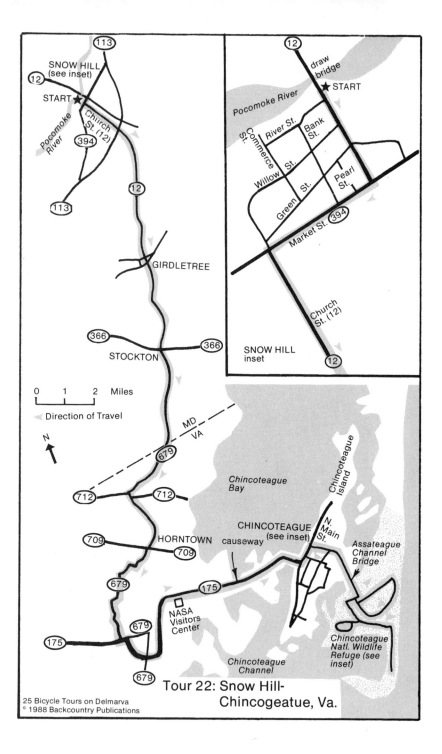

113

SNOW HILL
(see inset)

12 START

Pocomoke River

Church St. (12)

394

113

12

GIRDLETREE

366 **366**
STOCKTON

0   1   2   Miles

◀ Direction of Travel

N

MD
VA

679

712 **712**

709 HORNTOWN
709

679

175

NASA
Visitors
Center

679

175

679

Chincoteague
Bay

Chincoteague
Island

CHINCOTEAGUE
(see inset)
causeway

N. Main
St.

Assateague
Channel
Bridge

Chincoteague
Channel

Chincoteague
Natl. Wildlife
Refuge (see
inset)

**Tour 22: Snow Hill–
Chincogeatue, Va.**

25 Bicycle Tours on Delmarva
© 1988 Backcountry Publications

12
draw
bridge

★ START

Pocomoke River

Commerce
St.

River St.
Bank
St.

Willow
St.

Green
St.

Pearl
St.

Market St. **394**

Church
St. (12)

SNOW HILL
inset

12

24.4   **NASA Visitors Center.** You are now at the NASA/Wallops Facility of the Goddard Space Flight Center. This agency of the National Aeronautics and Space Administration has been here since 1945 and is concerned primarily with tracking space satellites and aircraft noise abatement. The Wallops Facility also conducts considerable research in space rocketry. The Visitors Center, which has many fine displays that chronicle the history of space research, is open five days a week, Thursday through Monday, 10:00 A.M. to 4:00 P.M.

29.2   **After crossing the long, narrow causeway across the Chincoteague Channel, enter the town of Chincoteague.** I left Snow Hill on a July morning at 10:00 A.M. and with stops and at a leisurely pace, I arrived in Chincoteague around 2:00 P.M. As there is much to see in the wildlife refuge, I recommend staying overnight at either a motel or campground. There are plenty of both kinds of facilities in the area.

After you have rested and found a place to stay, cycle out to the refuge; the best times in summer are in the early morning or late in the afternoon because of the heat.

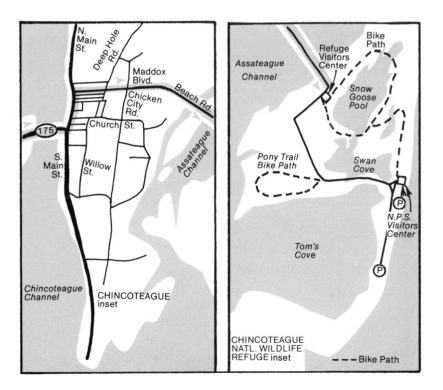

At the Chincoteague Channel Bridge, turn left and cycle up North Main Street. Turn right on Maddox Boulevard and proceed two miles to the Assateague Channel Bridge. This is the touristy part of Chincoteague; motels and restaurants have sprung up in abundance in the last few years. Just before the bridge is Tom's Cove Campground, a sprawling park and campground that can get quite crowded in summer.

Cross the Assateague Channel Bridge and follow the signs to the wildlife refuge bike path on the left. The bike paths of Chincoteague National Wildlife Refuge are, to put it mildly, wonderful! You can get away from the automobile traffic and become in tune with nature.

The park has two bike loops: The Snow Goose Pool Loop—3.5 miles; and The Pony Trail—1.5 miles. These loops take you through forest, marsh, and along tidewater pools of breathtaking beauty. Just don't daydream too much while you are communing with nature or you may collide with an occasional jogger. After you do both loops, follow the auto route to the beach and take a swim. There is a large bathhouse and Visitors Center at the beach, and there are steel bike racks so that you can secure your bicycle.

After a swim or a walk along part of the 12-mile wild beach, return to Chincoteague and splurge at one of the local ice-cream parlors.

A note for the return ride

As this tour is not a loop, you should arrange to be picked up by car or van after you have spent one night in Chincoteague. If you have the time and inclination, you may wish to pick up on Tour 24 and proceed to either Wachapreague or Cape Charles.

Bicycle repair services
None on this route.

Lodging
Birchwood Motel, South Main Street, Chincoteague, Virginia, (804) 336-6133.

23

Onancock Loop

Distance: 32.5 miles.
Terrain: Flat to rolling countryside, strong headwinds in autumn.
Location: Accomack County, Virginia
Special features: Onancock, Wachapreague, Accomac.

The town of Onancock, Virginia, on the Eastern Shore of the Chesapeake, is about 58 miles due south of Salisbury, Maryland. The drive down through Accomack County is worth the trip because you will encounter a 70-mile peninsula that is still unspoiled by tourism and commercial development. The Eastern Shore of Virginia moves at a pace much slower than the rest of Delmarva, and the names on the land like Pungoteague, Wachapreague, and Modest Town reflect the quaintness of the region. The two counties of the Virginia Eastern Shore, Accomack County and Northampton County, are large agricultural regions that encompass some 120,000 acres of crop land. Over 30,000 acres are planted annually in Irish potatoes. Large amounts of peppers, sweet potatoes, tomatoes, and snap beans are also grown.

The Eastern Shore of Virginia is one of the oldest settled regions in America. English colonists came here as early as 1620. Originally the region was referred to as Accomack Plantation, but by 1663 the two counties had been organized to give better political and economic coherence to the area. The Eastern Shore of Virginia was able to preserve much of its early charm because until the opening of the Chesapeake Bay Bridge-Tunnel in 1965, which connected the region with Norfolk and the rest of the state, Accomack and Northampton counties enjoyed relative isolation.

This tour begins in Onancock with good reason. First there are good overnight accommodations here. Second, you can, if you like, take an excursion boat from the wharf at Onancock to Tangier Island. While the ferry schedule is subject to change, you can get ticket and passenger information from Hopkins General Store and Restaurant at the wharf. Usually in summer *The Spirit of '76* sails from the wharf for Tangier Island at 10:00 A.M. and returns at 1:45 P.M. For ticket information call (804) 787-8220.

Directions for the ride

0.0. The loop begins at the wharf parking lot at Hopkins Restaurant in

Francis McKemie Memorial in Accomac, Virginia.

you can't get lost. Just follow any street to the water. The Wachapreague Marina Restaurant serves hot food at reasonable prices. Rest here awhile before continuing your loop.

16.7   Go back up Main Street and out of Wachapreague on Route 180.

17.6   Turn right on Route 605 for Accomac.

19.6   Chancetown, population 11, the smallest hamlet on the Eastern Shore of Virginia.

22.2   **Locustville and Locustville Academy.** Built in 1859 as a school for planters' children, the academy has been recently restored as an historic place.

24.2   Hamlet of Daugherty.

26.5   **Enter Accomac.** One of the most charming colonial villages on Virginia's Eastern Shore, Accomac is a photographer's delight. Accomac was settled as early as 1624 and its continuous court records date from 1632. Most of the houses in Accomac have been carefully restored and there is a kind of eighteenth-century ambiance to the town. The large frame houses with dormer windows and solid multiple chimneys are reminders of Accomac's prosperity as a legal and market center during the antebellum period.

26.7   At the stop sign turn right on Business Route 13.

26.9   At the intersection of Business Route 13 and Route 764 turn left. The Accomack County Court House will be on your left.

27.0   The Accomac Debtors Prison will be on your right. Built in 1784, this prison housed the county jailor and debtors from that date until the Virginia Legislature brought imprisonment for debt absolutely to an end in 1849.

      Retrace your route on Route 764 to the Court House and Business Route 13. At the intersection of Business Route 13 and Route 764, continue straight for a minitour of Accomac. You will now be on Route 1502.

27.2   At the stop sign turn right. The McKemie Presbyterian Church will be on your right.

27.3   Proceed one block to the stop sign. Turn right on Route 605.

27.4   Turn left onto Business Route 13.

28.4   Cross Route 13 and stay on Business Route 13. The Whispering Pines Motel will be on your right.

28.9   Enter Tasley.

29.5   At the stop sign you will be at the intersection of Route 13, Route 178, and Route 316. Go straight ahead on Route 178 west.

30.8   Enter Onancock.

30.9   At the stop sign turn right on Route 178 west and continue into Onancock.

32.5   Reach Onancock wharf and Hopkins Restaurant and General Store. Treat yourself to a cold drink as this is the end of your loop.

Bicycle repair services
None on this route.

Lodging
Colonial Manor Inn, 84 Market Street, Onancock, Virginia, (804) 787-3521.
The Spinning Wheel Bed & Breakfast, 21 North Street, Onancock, Virginia, (804) 787-7311.

A quaint road sign.

Two Chesapeake Centuries

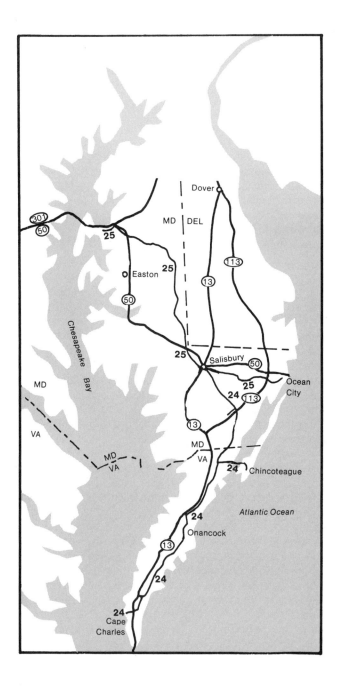

24

Salisbury, Maryland—Cape Charles, Virginia

Distance: 125 miles one way.
Time and distance planning: 3 days.
Salisbury, Maryland to Chincoteague, Virginia: 47 miles; Chincoteague to Wachapreague: 41 miles; Wachapreague to Cape Charles: 37 miles.
Terrain: Flat with occasional hills.
Location: Wicomico County and Worcester County, Maryland; Accomack County and Northampton County, Virginia.
Special features: Snow Hill, NASA Visitors Center, Chincoteague, Assateague Island, Wachapreague, Eastville, Cape Charles.

This 100-mile plus tour or century has been designed to introduce the cyclist to the lower Chesapeake region. Anyone who has an appreciation of the sea and eighteenth- and nineteenth-century architecture will enjoy a fascinating ride. The lower Eastern Shore of Maryland and Virginia is less commercialized and less visited than the rest of the Delmarva Peninsula, and it retains a kind of quaint southern charm and architectural distinctiveness that make it a worthwhile tour to the serious biker. This is a land of small fishing ports and tomato and potato farms. On the lower Eastern Shore the Old South is not a memory. It is everyday life for an historically rooted, confident, and gentle people.

With the exception of Route 175, the causeway to Chincoteague, automobile traffic is very light on the route suggested. I have scheduled three days for this tour with destinations that have motel accommodations. The distances are deliberately under fifty miles per day because many of you will be biking this route in summer. Often during torrid summer days on the Delmarva Peninsula fifty miles can seem like five hundred.

This tour begins at the corner of Camden Avenue and College Avenue at the campus of Salisbury State College in Salisbury. From the college, the ride proceeds along Route 12 to Snow Hill and then on Route 679 to Wattsville, Virginia, and the Chincoteague cutoff. On the second day, return to Wattsville and continue on Route 679 to Modest Town. From Modest Town take Route 187 and cross Route 13 for Bloxom, Virginia. At Bloxom follow Route 316 to Greenbush. From Greenbush take Route 764 to Accomac. From Accomac take the Wachapreague Road, Route 605.

Outside of Wachapreague, on the third day, you will take Route 600, which goes to Cheriton and Cape Charles.

This is strictly a one-way trip. Once you arrive at Cape Charles you should plan on being picked up by van or car if you wish to return to Salisbury. Should you wish to continue south, you will have to take a bus with your bicycle through the Chesapeake Bay Bridge-Tunnel. (No cyclists are permitted on the bridge-tunnel.) You can catch an intercity bus either north or south at Paul's Restaurant in the village of Cheriton, Virginia.

Directions for the ride
Day One: Salisbury to Chincoteague

0.0 College Avenue and Camden Avenue at Salisbury State College. Proceed east on College Avenue across Route 13 and pass the Dresser-Wayne Pump Company on your right.

1.4 Turn right on Route 12/Snow Hill Road.

7.3 Worcester County line. Once you cross the county line the road gets wider.

13.9 Iron Furnace Road.
   Side trip: If you wish, turn right here for a 4-mile diversion to the historic Nassawango Iron Furnace (see Tour 20).

17.5 Enter Snow Hill (see Tour 21).

17.9 Cross the Pocomoke River. If you are looking for a few hours of lazy canoeing on the river or exploring the great Pocomoke Swamp, you can hire equipment as well as a guide at the Pocomoke River Canoe Company, which has headquarters located right at the bridge. (Open on weekends in fall and spring, daily from Memorial Day to Labor Day, (301) 632-3971.)

18.1 Turn right at the traffic light onto Market Street.

18.2 Turn left on Church Street/Route 12 to Girdletree and Stockton.

19.7 At the intersection and stop sign at Route 113, cross Route 113 and continue on Route 12.

24.0 Enter Girdletree. There is a good country store here for cold drinks and snacks.

27.0 Enter Stockton.

27.5 In Stockton pass Flemings Grocery Store at the crossroads of Route 366 and Route 12. Continue south on Route 12.

30.9 At the Virginia State line Route 12 becomes Route 679. Continue on Route 679 south.

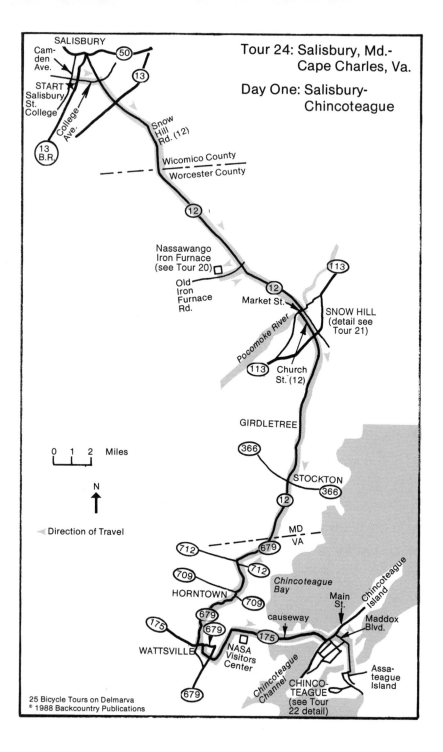

SALISBURY

Cam-
den
Ave.

50

13

START
Salisbury
St.
College

College Ave.

13
B.R.

Snow
Hill
Rd. (12)

Wicomico County
Worcester County

12

Nassawango
Iron Furnace
(see Tour 20)

Old
Iron
Furnace
Rd.

12

113

Market St.

SNOW HILL
(detail see
Tour 21)

Pocomoke River

113

Church
St. (12)

GIRDLETREE

366

STOCKTON

366

12

0 1 2 Miles

N

◄ Direction of Travel

MD
VA

712

679

712

709

HORNTOWN

709

Chincoteague
Bay

Main
St.

Chincoteague
Island

175

679

679

WATTSVILLE

NASA
Visitors
Center

causeway

175

Maddox
Blvd.

Assa-
teague
Island

Chincoteague
Channel

CHINCO-
TEAGUE
(see Tour
22 detail)

679

25 Bicycle Tours on Delmarva
© 1988 Backcountry Publications

Tour 24: Salisbury, Md.-
Cape Charles, Va.

Day One: Salisbury-
Chincoteague

34.7 Horntown, Virginia.

38.9 At the intersection of Route 679 and Route 175 turn left onto Route 175 for Chincoteague Island. Stop at Coffin's Market for cold drinks and excellent homemade sandwiches.

42.3 NASA Visitors Center. The Wallops Island Facility, as it is known locally, was involved in American space research and rocketry in the 1950s long before "Space" was news. NASA does important weather and satellite research here. The Visitors Center is open Thursday through Monday.

As you cross the Route 175 causeway to Chincoteague, proceed with the utmost caution. Summer traffic is heavy and the two-lane road has no shoulder for cyclists.

47.7 Main Street, Chincoteague Island. See Tour 22 for information on Chincoteague and Assateague.

Day Two: Chincoteague to Wachapreague

55.4 Backtrack from Chincoteague Island to the intersection of Route 175 and Route 679. Turn left on Route 679, heading south.

57.8 Atlantic. Not as sleepy as it looks, the village of Atlantic has several stores and an excellent pharmacy located nearby on Route 13.

65.8 Enter Modest Town. The village's name says it all.

66.5 Leave Modest Town passing the large Modest Town Baptist Church on your right. Turn right on Route 187.

67.6 Cross Route 13 at Nelsonia and continue on Route 187 to Bloxom.

69.2 Enter Bloxom and you have entered the Deep South of Virginia's Eastern Shore. You'll see some depressing poverty on the outskirts of town. Bloxom is a slow-moving country town whose ways and habits are not always fathomable to outsiders. With thousands of acres in the area planted in tomatoes and other truck crops, Bloxom is an important migrant labor center so you may hear some Spanish spoken. Stop at the local coffee shop at the corner of Route 187 and Route 316. Virginia Shoremen are friendly and curious about long-distance cyclists.

69.8 Turn left on Route 316, which runs due south parallel to the Eastern Shore Railroad tracks.

73.0 Enter Parksley, a Victorian gem. It is a flourishing little town with clean streets and well-kept homes.

76.9 At Greenbush turn left on Route 764 for Accomac.

78.1 Cross Route 13 and enter Accomac, the county seat of Accomack County. The Shore Stop convenience market at this intersection is the

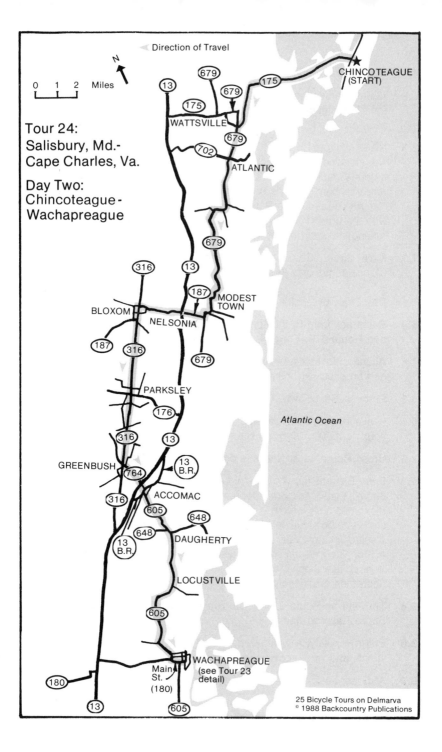

Direction of Travel

N

0 1 2 Miles

Tour 24:
Salisbury, Md.-
Cape Charles, Va.

Day Two:
Chincoteague-
Wachapreague

CHINCOTEAGUE
(START)

679
679
175
13
175
WATTSVILLE
679
702
ATLANTIC

679

316
13
187
MODEST
TOWN
BLOXOM
NELSONIA
187
316
679

PARKSLEY
176
Atlantic Ocean

316
13
GREENBUSH
13
B.R.
764
ACCOMAC
316
605
648
648
DAUGHERTY
13
B.R.

LOCUSTVILLE

605

180
WACHAPREAGUE
Main (see Tour 23
St. detail)
(180)
13
605

25 Bicycle Tours on Delmarva
© 1988 Backcountry Publications

only place in Accomac to buy a sandwich, drink, or supplies. The local restaurant and store in town was purchased by county lawyers and turned into offices.

78.6   **Accomac Debtors' Prison is on your left.** This building was originally the eighteenth-century residence of the county jailer before being converted into a debtors' prison in 1842.

   Side trip: For a brief diversion, proceed straight ahead past the courthouse and across Business Route 13. The mansion of antebellum governor Henry A. Wise will be on your right. At the memorial to Reverend Francis McKemie, the founder of Presbyterianism on the Eastern Shore in the seventeenth century, turn left onto a shady lane. Many of the old colonial homes of Accomac have been lovingly restored, and Accomac still appears much like an English country village. Turn left on Business Route 13 to resume your mileage count from the courthouse.

78.8   **Turn left on Route 605/Wachapreague Road.** Note the splendid multi-chimney house on your left.

A country house in Accomac, Virginia.

80.7 Village of Daugherty.

83.2 Enter Locustville. When I last rode through here, this hamlet had a sign that boasted Locustville's population of 11. The Methodist Church is on your right. The old Locustville Academy (1859) on your left is worth a look as well.

87.8 Turn left at the stop sign onto Route 180 for Wachapreague.

88.3 Enter Wachapreague and proceed down Main Street.

Wachapreague is the fishing capital of Virginia's Eastern Shore. Its docks are full of charter fishing boats and the flounder fishing here in summer is the best around. The boats go out early in the morning, and at 5:00 A.M. the town is abuzz with activity. At the marina restaurant you can eat well on a budget and swap fish stories with the locals. At the Wachapreague Motel you can rent an outboard motor boat for the day and explore Parramore and Cedar islands, the barrier island haunts of the famous sixteenth-century pirate, Blackbeard. Later in the day sit in the Island House Restaurant and watch the boats come in.

Day Three: Wachapreague to Cape Charles

88.7 Leave Wachapreague on Route 180.

91.6 Turn left (south) onto Route 600. Route 600 parallels Route 13 south. It is a farm road to Nassawadox and Cheriton, and you will find no country stores or service stations on this route.

115.1 **Side trip:** At the intersection of Route 600 and Route 631, take a 1.3-mile diversion on Route 631 to Eastville, the seat of Northampton County to visit the oldest courthouse in Virginia still in use. Close by are old antebellum law offices (one-room buildings) still used by Northampton County lawyers. Eastville is the smallest county seat on the Eastern Shore and has a population of 238.

Northampton County was one of the first eight shires created in Virginia in 1634 and originally called Accomac. In 1643 the Virginia Eastern Shore was divided into two political units—Accomack County to the north and Northampton to the south. Northampton County played an important part in maintaining the first permanent English settlement at Jamestown by providing salt and meat to the settlement during its early existence. The old courthouse dates from 1730 and has the oldest court records in America. Have lunch in the historic Eastville Inn. Return to Route 600 to the point of diversion, turn right (south), and resume your mileage count.

119.6 At the intersection of Route 600 and Route 639 turn right on Route 639 for Cheriton.

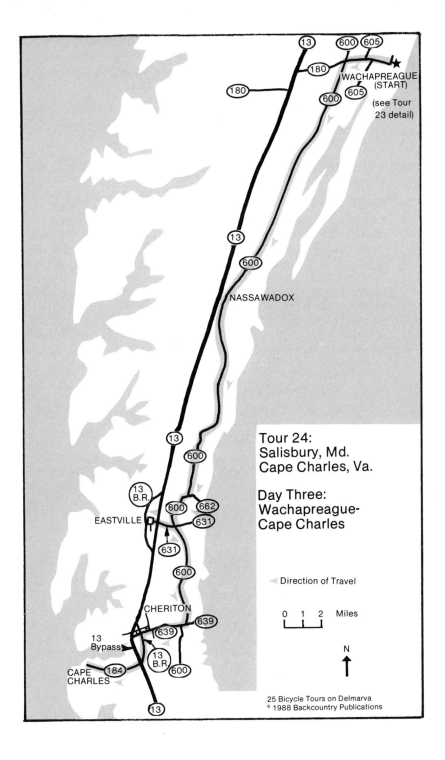

13

600

605

180

180

600

605

WACHAPREAGUE
(START)

(see Tour
23 detail)

13

600

NASSAWADOX

13

600

13
B.R.

600

662

631

EASTVILLE

631

600

CHERITON

639

639

13
Bypass

13
B.R.

600

CAPE
CHARLES

184

13

Tour 24:
Salisbury, Md.
Cape Charles, Va.

Day Three:
Wachapreague-
Cape Charles

Direction of Travel

0   1   2   Miles

N

25 Bicycle Tours on Delmarva
© 1988 Backcountry Publications

121.0   **Enter Cheriton,** a flourishing agribusiness center with an intercity bus stop at Paul's Restaurant on Business Route 13.

121.9   In Cheriton, turn left on Business Route 13 and proceed south out of town.

122.8   Cross Route 13 and take Route 184 to Cape Charles.

124.6   Enter Cape Charles and continue straight ahead on Randolph Avenue to the bay.

125.0   **Cape Charles Beach, gazebo, and promenade.** Cape Charles was established in 1884 when the New York, Philadelphia, and Norfolk Railroad extended its service from Philadelphia to Norfolk. Cape Charles flourished as a rail and passenger ferry port and became the largest town in Northampton County. The opening of the Chesapeake Bay Bridge-Tunnel in 1965 put an end to Cape Charles' ferry industry and today the town is a bit down at the heels. The town beach and promenade are still lovely, though. From here you have the rare opportunity in the East to see the sun set over water. Congratulations on the end of your century!

Bicycle repair services

Salisbury Schwinn Cyclery, 1404 South Salisbury Boulevard, Salisbury, Maryland, (410) 546-4747.

The Bikesmith, 1503 North Salisbury Boulevard, Salisbury, Maryland, (410) 749-2453.

Lodging

Temple Hill Motel, South Salisbury Boulevard, (.50 mile south of Salisbury State College), Salisbury, Maryland, (301) 742-3284.

Birchwood Motel, Main Street, Chincoteague, Virginia, (804) 336-6133.

Wachapreague Motel, Main Street, Wachapreague, Virginia, (804) 787-2105.

Rittenhouse Motor Lodge, (.50 mile south of Route 13-Cape Charles Interchange), Cheriton, Virginia, (804) 331-2768.

25

Kent Narrows—Ocean City, Maryland

Distance: 110 miles.
Time and distance planning: 2 days.
　　Kent Narrows to Salisbury: 73 miles; Salisbury to Ocean City: 37 miles.
Terrain: Rolling farmlands.
Location: Queen Anne's County, Caroline County, Dorchester County, Wicomico County, and Worcester County, Maryland.
Special features: Kent Narrows, Wye Mills, Wye Oak, Martinak State Park, Salisbury, Berlin, Ocean City.

This tour has been designed specifically to get the cyclist to the beach at Ocean City without fighting summer and holiday traffic all the way to the sea from Kent Island. It is not the most direct route, but it is certainly the safest and most scenic. As there are few accommodations along this route, I suggest that you attempt to cycle to Salisbury in one day.

On the Kent Narrows–Salisbury leg of your journey you will cross miles of open countryside, and the lack of shaded roads in summer makes for a sweltering ride. Make provisions for hot weather cycling. When we took this route, my son Stewart and I left Kent Narrows at dawn in order to take advantage of a cool July morning. In the afternoon, however, we were forced by the heat to take frequent stops for rest and water.

From Salisbury to Ocean City the countryside is more varied and more shaded. The country stores of Powellville are worth a visit, Berlin is full of country bustle, and Ocean City froths with its mixture of neon, Coney Island, condominium glitz, and tourist hustle.

Directions for the ride

0.0　　This tour begins at Kent Narrows on Route 18 at the parking lot of the Angler's Restaurant. To get to the restaurant/starting point, take Route 50 east by car from Annapolis and go to the end of Kent Island. Take the first right after the Kent Narrows drawbridge. At the intersection turn right on Route 18 and proceed to the restaurant. Route 18 allows you to avoid the hectic traffic of Route 50 and to experience the more relaxed atmosphere of marinas and seafood houses. In the morning at Kent Narrows you can watch elegant yachts and fishing vessels waiting for the bridge to rise so they can proceed outward to Eastern Bay and the pleasant waters of the Wye River. **Mount your bike at the Angler's**

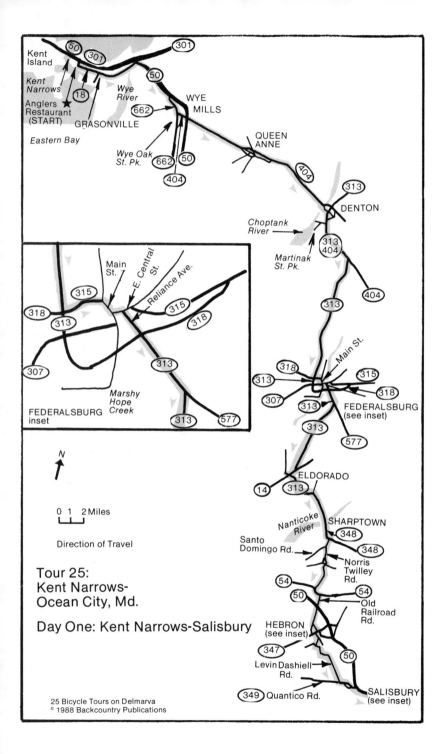

Kent
Island

Kent
Narrows

Anglers
Restaurant
(START)

GRASONVILLE

Eastern Bay

50
301
301

50

18

Wye
River

WYE
MILLS

662

Wye Oak
St. Pk.

662 50

404

QUEEN
ANNE

404

313

DENTON

Choptank
River

313
404

Martinak
St. Pk.

404

313

Main St.

318

313

307

307

318

313

Main St.

318

315

318

313

FEDERALSBURG
(see inset)

577

Main
St.

E. Central
St.

Reliance Ave.

315

318

315

318

313

Marshy
Hope
Creek

FEDERALSBURG
inset

313

577

N

0 1 2 Miles

Direction of Travel

Tour 25:
Kent Narrows-
Ocean City, Md.

Day One: Kent Narrows-Salisbury

ELDORADO

14

313

Nanticoke
River

SHARPTOWN

348

348

Santo
Domingo Rd.

Norris
Twilley
Rd.

54

54

50

Old
Railroad
Rd.

HEBRON
(see inset)

347

Levin Dashiell
Rd.

349 Quantico Rd.

50

SALISBURY
(see inset)

25 Bicycle Tours on Delmarva
© 1988 Backcountry Publications

Restaurant and head east on Route 18.

1.2   **Enter the village of Grasonville** where there are "juntique" shops and general stores for you to explore. Grasonville is rapidly entering the suburban orbit of Annapolis, and the traffic on Route 18 can be busy at times.

5.3   **At the junction with Route 50, turn right onto Route 50.** Unfortunately a

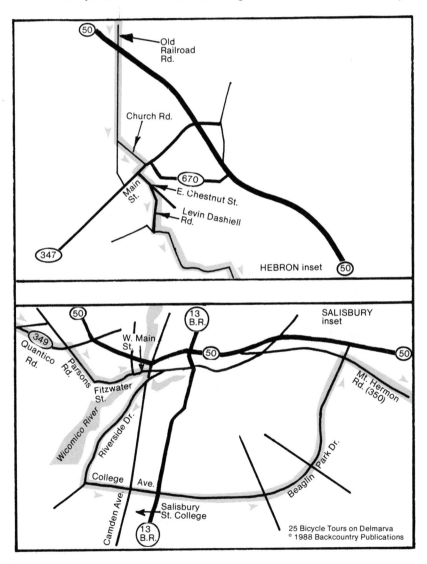

25 Bicycle Tours on Delmarva
© 1988 Backcountry Publications

small stretch of biking on this four-lane highway can't be avoided. **Proceed with caution.**

9.7   Exit Route 50 and turn right onto Route 662. This relatively deserted stretch of country highway will take you to Wye Mills.

11.1 **Enter Wye Mills.** A gristmill has stood on this site since the early eighteenth century. Flour ground here was shipped to General Washington's troops during the American Revolution. Though Wye Mills appears to be a sleepy village, it boasts a summer playhouse that produces musicals and serious drama and has a community college, Chesapeake College.

   Side trip: Continue 1.2 miles on Route 662 and you will come to Wye Oak, the most famous tree in Maryland. Believed to be over 400 years old, Wye Oak is 104 feet high and has a trunk 32 feet in circumference. Both the tree and an acre and a half of land have been acquired by the state as a park. The best way to photograph Wye Oak and its nearby colonial house is from the parking lot of the feed mill directly across the road from the tree.

   The Old Wye Church that is nearby is an elegant eighteenth-century Episcopal chapel that has been completely restored. For a taste of the local history, try Chesapeake Beaten Biscuits sold next door at Orell's Bakery. Made from the old colonial recipe, the beaten biscuit was a staple during lean times and transatlantic voyages. It does not have a shelf life, it has a half life.

11.1 From Wye Oak backtrack to Route 404 in the village of Wye Mills and go right on Route 404 east.

12.2 At the intersection of Route 404 and Route 50, cross Route 50 and proceed east on Route 404. The "404" is a favorite with many bikers because it is a quick way to get to the beaches of southern Delaware. Once the 404 enters Delaware, it becomes an exceedingly unsafe road. I do not recommend it because the Delaware section of Route 404 is clogged with summer traffic, has little or no shoulder for cyclists, and is poorly maintained by the state. I believe that the 404 is safe only as far as the cutoff at Route 313 to Federalsburg.

24.2 Continuing on Route 404 east, exit at Denton for downton Denton. The road briefly becomes four lanes at the approach of the Choptank River Bridge. Go straight across the bridge on Route 404.

25.4 **Enter Denton,** the seat of Caroline County. Denton is the kind of Eastern Shore town that still thrills to firemen's parades, summer band concerts, and Fourth of July celebrations.

25.7 **The Denton Court House** sits dreamily in the middle of a shaded lawn, and old timers sit on park benches and watch traffic go by. Denton was once a major tomato cannery center and steamboat landing. In summer, take time to savor the fresh cantaloupes and vegetables sold locally at roadside stands.

25.8 **Turn left at the stop sign onto Franklin Street/Route 404.** In Denton, Route 404 is one way in each direction.

27.7 **Martinak State Park** sits on the upper reachs of the Choptank River. This is a good place to take a picnic lunch break and visit a log cabin museum of Indian artifacts.

31.2 **Turn right on Route 313 and head south to Federalsburg.**

41.3 For such a small town, the traffic pattern of Federalsburg can be confusing. **You can bypass Federalsburg by swinging around the town on Route 313. Or you can turn left and enter the town at the traffic light on Route 315.** Federalsburg is larger than one would expect for such a rural area. The main streets and shops have a 1950s quality to them. Most people work in local canneries, food processing plants, or in the textile mills of the DuPont Corporation in nearby Seaford, Delaware.

42.1 **In Federalsburg, turn right on Bloomingdale Avenue, which becomes Main Street.**

42.4 **Turn left on East Central Street.**

42.6 **Turn right on Reliance Avenue. This will be the first right turn after crossing the bridge across Marshy Hope Creek.**

43.1 **At the traffic light and intersection of Route 318 and Route 313, continue on Route 313 south.**

44.3 **Keep right on Route 313 and enter Dorchester County.**

51.2 **Enter Eldorado.** The name of this hamlet is more romantic than its appearance. **At Eldorado keep left on Route 313.**

56.5 **Cross the Nanticoke River on a new bridge. At the end of the bridge, turn right and enter Sharptown.** Until World War II, Sharptown was a booming agricultural village and ship construction center. While time has passed it by, it still has a pickle factory, a country and western bar, and residents who think their village is the center of the universe. The local bar is friendly and serves ketchup-flavored potato chips. The locals are curious and friendly and love to talk about crabbing and fishing. In summer you can smell crabs being steamed with Old Bay Seasoning on village stoves.

56.7 **Turn left on Ferry Street.**

57.0 **At the blinker light, turn left on Route 348.**

58.2   **Turn right onto Santo Domingo Road.** (Interestingly many refugee French planters from Haiti settled in Maryland after the black nationalist slave revolt led by Toussaint Louverture in the 1790s. The old name for Haiti, Santo Domingo, is now part of the Maryland landscape.)

58.8   **Turn left onto Norris Twilley Road. Caution:** Norris Twilley is unpaved but navigable for two miles.

62.6   Reach the end of Norris Twilley Road. At the stop sign turn left onto Route 54.

63.3   Turn right onto Old Railroad Road, heading south.

64.1   Cross Route 50 and continue south.

65.7   Turn left onto Church Road and proceed to Hebron.

66.2   **Enter Hebron.** An old railroad village dating from the 1890s, Hebron has quiet back streets and roads. The town has a large grocery store and a restaurant for weary and hungry cyclists.

66.3   Turn right on Main Street. Go past the IGA Supermarket that will be on your right.

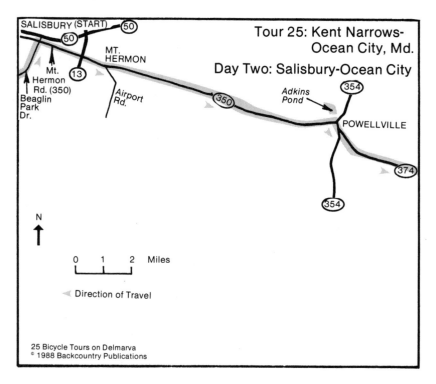

Tour 25: Kent Narrows-Ocean City, Md.
Day Two: Salisbury-Ocean City

N

0   1   2   Miles

◁ Direction of Travel

25 Bicycle Tours on Delmarva
© 1988 Backcountry Publications

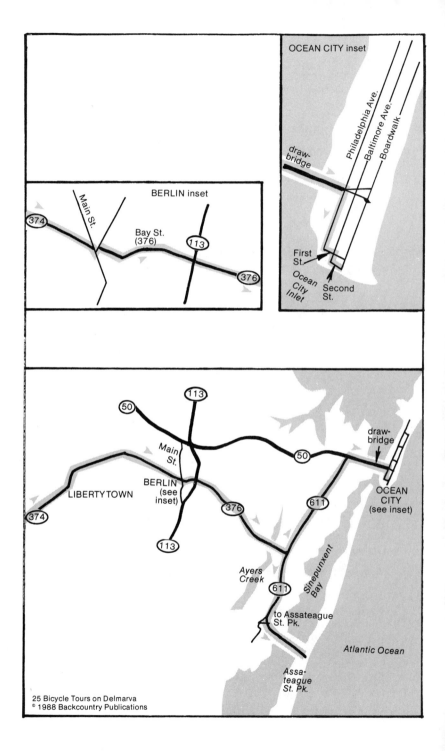

OCEAN CITY inset

Philadelphia Ave.

Baltimore Ave.

Boardwalk

draw-
bridge

First
St.

Ocean
City
Inlet

Second
St.

BERLIN inset

Main St.

Bay St.
(376)

374

113

376

113

50

Main
St.

draw-
bridge

50

LIBERTYTOWN

BERLIN
(see
inset)

376

611

OCEAN
CITY
(see inset)

374

113

Ayers
Creek

611

Sinepuxent
Bay

to Assateague
St. Pk.

Atlantic Ocean

Assa-
teague
St. Pk.

25 Bicycle Tours on Delmarva
© 1988 Backcountry Publications

66.5 Turn left on East Chestnut Street at the Hebron carnival grounds. (Like many towns here on the Eastern Shore, the Volunteer Fire Department of Hebron hosts a carnival each year to raise money to buy equipment.)

66.7 Turn right onto Levin Dashiell Road.

71.5 Reach the end of Levin Dashiell Road. At the stop sign turn left onto Quantico Road/Route 349. Enter Salisbury.

Salisbury is the largest town on the Eastern Shore with a metropolitan population in excess of 60,000. It has been a major port in the region since the 1790s and ranks after Baltimore and Crisfield for ship freight tonnage in the state. Recently economic growth, particularly in the service sector, has transformed Salisbury from a farming center of feed mills and fertilizer plants to an important medical, legal, and food processing center. Salisbury is the home of Perdue Chicken Inc. and the capital of the entire Delmarva broiler industry. Its growth, however, has not detracted from its being a very liveable urban center, and cyclists can enjoy the parks and city zoo. Even more important, cyclists can move in and out of Salisbury with little difficulty as traffic, even in rush hour, has yet to become bothersome.

72.5 Turn right on Parsons Road and pass Prestige Autos on your right. As you approach the crest of a hill you will overlook a shipyard.

73.0 Parsons Road becomes Fitzwater Street, then West Main Street. The flourishing shipyard makes a stark contrast to the substandard neighborhood.

73.5 Continue on West Main and cross the small steel drawbridge. Turn right at the traffic light. Bear right on Riverside Drive. The Wicomico River will be on your right. Continue on Riverside Drive.

74.6 Turn left on College Avenue and continue straight through the intersection/traffic light of Camden Avenue and College Avenue. Salisbury State College will be on your right. Cross Route 13, continuing on College Avenue, which becomes Beaglin Park Drive.

78.0 Turn right on Mt. Hermon Road/Route 350.

80.4 Pass through the hamlet of Mt. Hermon. At the intersection of Airport Road (nearby is Salisbury's Airport with passenger service to Baltimore and Washington) and Ward's Cash Market, continue on Route 350 through the Wicomico County Nature Preserve. Stop along the way to enjoy the cool shade and the wildfowl life of the perserve.

88.4 Enter Powellville. Boasting two general stores, Powellville is an excellent resting place. The stores serve coffee and sandwiches. Cycle over to the nearby dam and relax at Adkins Pond for a while.

89.0 At the intersection of Route 350 and Route 354, turn right on Route 354. The countryside is very pretty through here. Enjoy the patches of shade on the road.

89.4 Turn left on Route 374. If you miss this turn for Ocean City, you will end up in Snow Hill.

94.1 Pass through the hamlet of Libertytown.

98.7 Enter Berlin, a shady pleasant town. Its winding streets contain many interesting colonial and Victorian homes and the business section is compact and prosperous.

99.5 Take care not to miss the Bay Street turn. At Main Street and Farlow's Pharmacy, make a sharp right turn, then left at the Peninsula Bank. Bear right on Bay Street/Route 376.

99.9 There is a traffic light at the intersection of Route 113 and Route 376. Continue on Route 376.

103.4 At **Ayers Creek Bridge** you have a lovey waterfront vista. Often you will see people on the bridge fishing and catching crabs.

104.1 At the junction of Route 376 and Route 611 you have two options. **Side trip:** You can turn right and follow Route 611 to Assateague Park and its beaches. After three miles you will come to a large bridge that will take you across Sinepuxent Bay to Assateague Island. The island is a great sandbar whose permanent residents are waterfowl and wild ponies that have been there since Spanish galleons wrecked off the coast in the sixteenth century. The area is still wild and is very popular with back-packers, sports fishermen, and campers. Although it is fun to walk along the dunes and to swim at the state beach at Assateague, bear in mind that there is no shade on the island and the sand roads are difficult to navigate on a bicycle. Still, you have 35 miles of undeveloped beach to stroll along to search for sand dollars and other interesting shells. There is a public campground at Assateague State Park. For further information contact Assateague National Seashore, Route 2, Box 294, Berlin, Maryland 21811, (301) 641-1441. (If you have never camped out on an open beach before, mind the sand flies!)

   If you choose the other option, turn left and proceed to Ocean City. **Caution:** Route 611 is busy in summer, especially where it passes Ocean City Airport.

108.1 At the intersection of Route 611 and Route 50, turn right onto Route 50. Cross the drawbridge into Ocean City. Because of the heavy resort traffic on the bridge, use the sidewalk. The bridge sidewalk is fenced off to protect walkers, bikers, and fishermen.

110.0   After the bridge, turn right on Philadelphia Avenue and proceed to the
Ocean City inlet and the Ocean City Lifesaving Museum. You will now
be at the water's edge on First Street. This is a pretty part of the resort,
and the beach here is wide. Despite the strong currents at the inlet, there
is plenty of boat traffic and there is always a throng of people fishing from
the large stone jetty.

A few comments about Ocean City will suffice: some will see Ocean
City as a noisy seaside honky tonk run amuck with neon commercial
development. Others see a popular family resort with boardwalk prom-
enades, food stands, and amusements for children. I prefer the old part
of Ocean City near the inlet to the high-rise Gold Coast to the north.

Ocean City has been a resort since 1872. With the coming of the
railroad and the construction of a bridge to the mainland, Ocean City
boomed, and it has never stopped booming. The town has always been
the home of slick promoters and real estate speculators. Please note that
Ocean City does have a crime problem in summer, mostly with petty
theft, so please keep a sharp eye on your bicycle.

The Lifesaving Museum in Ocean City.

Despite my personal cynicism about the place, I have enjoyed my visits to Ocean City. Cycling on the boardwalk provides a glorious ride at dawn when the surf is breaking. In season, cycling is permitted on the boardwalk until 10:00 A.M. I have also enjoyed the clean beaches, which are well patrolled by excellent lifeguards. And, if you are a youthful, blithe spirit, nothing beats the social action of Ocean City.

Bicycle repair services
Continental Cycles, 7203 Coastal Highway, Ocean City, Maryland, (410) 524-1313.

Lodging
Sophie Kerr House, Route 3, Box 7-B, Denton, Maryland, (410) 479-3421.
Temple Hill Motel, Route 13 and Kay Avenue, Salisbury, Maryland, (410) 742-3284.
Econo-Lodge, 102 60th Street, Ocean City, Maryland, (410) 524-5634.

Appendix #1
General Information on Travel and Tourism

Maryland's Eastern Shore

Cecil County, Office of Economic Development, County Office Building, Room 300, Elkton, Maryland 21921, (301) 398-0200, Ext. 144.

Kent County Chamber of Commerce, P.O. Box 146, 118 N. Cross Street, Chestertown, Maryland 21620, (301) 778-0416.

Talbot County Chamber of Commerce, P.O. Box 1366, Easton, Maryland 21601, (301) 822-4606.

Dorchester County Tourism, P.O. Box 307, Cambridge, Maryland 21613, (301) 228-3234.

Somerset County Tourism, P.O. Box 243, Princess Anne, Maryland, 21853.

Ocean City Visitors Bureau, Box 116 (OTD), Ocean City, Maryland 21842, (301) 289-8181.

Southern Delaware

Lewes Chamber of Commerce, P.O. Box 1, Lewes, Delaware 19958, (302) 645-8073.

New Castle Court House, Delaware Street, New Castle, Delaware 19720, (302) 323-4453.

Rehoboth Beach Chamber of Commerce, P.O. Box 216, Rehoboth Beach, Delaware 19971, (800) 441-1329.

Eastern Shore of Virginia

Chincoteague Chamber of Commerce, P.O. Box 258, Chincoteague, Virginia 23336, (804) 336-6161.

New Jersey

Cape May Chamber of Commerce, P.O. Box 74, Cape May Court House, Cape May, New Jersey 08210, (609) 465-7181.

Appendix #2
Inns and Bed and Breakfast
Accommodations

Bed and Breakfast accommodations are not to be confused with private inns or guest houses. Usually these B&Bs are in private homes. The great advantage of these accommodations is good price, congenial surroundings, and hosts who care about their guests. Should you require a B&B during one of your cycle trips in the Chesapeake, the following agencies can arrange a booking for you:

Maryland
The Traveller in Maryland, 33 West Street, Annapolis, Maryland 21401, (301) 269-6232.
Amanda's Reservation Service, 1428 Park Avenue, Baltimore, Maryland 21217, (301) 225-0001.

Virginia
Bed and Breakfast of Tidewater Virginia, Box 3343, Norfolk, Virginia 23514, (804) 627-1983.

Delaware
Bed and Breakfast of Delaware, 1804 Breen Lane, Wilmington, Delaware 19810, (302) 479-9500.

The following is a list of inns that welcome cyclists and participate in inn-to-inn bicycle-touring packages:

Delaware
Spring Garden Bed and Breakfast, Route 1, Box 283A, Delaware Avenue Extended, Laurel, Delaware 19956, (302) 875-7015.
The Towers, 101 NW Front Street, Milford, Delaware 19963, (302) 422-3814.
The Banking House, 112 NW Front Street, Milford, Delaware 19963, (302) 422-5708.
Ganvier-Black House B&B, 17 The Strand, New Castle, Delaware 19720, (302) 328-1339.

Maryland

Nanticocke Manor House, Church Street and Water Street, Vienna, Maryland 21869, (301) 376-3530.

Holland House, 5 Bay Street, Berlin, Maryland 21811, (301) 641-1956.

The Tavern House, 111 Water Street, Box 98, Vienna, Maryland 21869, (301) 376-3347.

The Bishop's House Bed and Breakfast, P.O. Box 2217, 214 Goldsborough Street, Easton, Maryland 21601, (301) 820-7290.

Hayman House c. 1898, 117 Prince William Street, Princess Anne, Maryland 21853, (301) 651-2753.

Inn at the Canal, 104 Bohemia Avenue, Chesapeake City, Maryland 21915, (301) 885-5995.

Commodore's Cottage, 215 Glenburn Avenue, Cambridge, Maryland 21613, (301) 228-6938.

Two Swan Inn, Foot Carpenter Street, P.O. Box 727, St. Michaels, Maryland 21663, (301) 745-2929.

John S. McDaniel House, 14 N. Aurora Street, Easton, Maryland 21601, (301) 822-3704.

Brampton Bed & Breakfast, RR 2, Box 107, Chestertown, Maryland 21620, (301) 778-1832.

Lantern Inn, 115 Ericsson Avenue, P.O. Box 29, Betterton, Maryland 21610, (301) 348-5809.

For more information about the packages these inns provide, contact Gwen North, Spring Garden Bed and Breakfast, Route 1, Box 283A, Delaware Avenue Extended, Laurel, Delaware 19956, (302) 875-7015.

Appendix #3
Bicycle Camping in Chesapeake Bay Country

Many of you will be cycling in the Chesapeake during good weather in either spring or summer. Camping offers an inexpensive and very enjoyable alternative to staying in costly inns or motels. Because of weight limitations, keep your gear to the basics: small two-man tent, sleeping bag, ground cloth, and eating utensils.

These campgrounds are listed in accordance with the tours that you may be taking on the Eastern Shore.

Tour 2, Tour 3, Tour 4.
Duck Neck Campground, RD#1, Box 262, Chestertown, Maryland 21620, (301) 778-3070.

Tour 5, Tour 6, Tour 7.
Cape Henlopen State Park, Lewes, Delaware, 19958, (302) 875-7543.

Tour 13, Tour 25.
Assateague National Seashore, Route 2, Box 294, Berlin, Maryland 21811, (301) 641-1441.

Tour 15, Tour 16, Tour 17.
Princess Anne Campground, Box 427, Princess Anne, Maryland 21853, (301) 651-1520.

Tour 18, Tour 19.
Janes Island State Park, Crisfield, Maryland 21817, (301) 968-1565.

Tour 22, Tour 24.
Tom's Cove Camp Ground, P.O. Box 122, Chincoteague Island, Virginia 23336, (804) 336-6498.

Also from Backcountry Publications and The Countryman Press

Regional Bicycling Guides

25 Bicycle Tours in Maryland, $12.00
25 Bicycle Tours in and around Washington, D.C., $10.00
25 Bicycle Tours in New Jersey, $10.00
25 Bicycle Tours in Eastern Pennsylvania, $10.00
25 Bicycle Tours in the Texas Hill Country and West Texas, $13.00
25 Bicycle Tours in Coastal Georgia and the Carolina Low Country, $12.00
30 Bicycle Tours in Wisconsin, $13.00
25 Bicycle Tours in Southern Indiana, $10.95
25 Bicycle Tours in Ohio's Western Reserve, $12.00
20 Bicycle Tours in and around New York City, $9.00
20 Bicycle Tours in the Five Boroughs, $8.95
20 Bicycle Tours in the Finger Lakes, $10.00
The Bicyclist's Guide to the Southern Berkshires, $14.95
30 Bicycle Tours in New Hampshire, $11.00
25 Bicycle Tours in Vermont, $11.00
25 Bicycle Tours in Maine, $10.00
25 Mountain Bike Tours in Massachusetts, $11.00
25 Mountain Bike Tours in Vermont, $11.00

Other Books about Delmarva & vicinity

Walks and Rambles on the Delmarva Peninsula, $11.00
50 Hikes in New Jersey, $13.00
50 Hikes in Northern Virginia, $13.00
50 Hikes in North Carolina, $14.00
50 Hikes in Eastern Pennsylvania, $12.00
Best Festivals Mid-Atlantic, $13.00
Food Festival, $16.00
New Jersey's Special Places, $14.00
Virgnia Trout Streams, $15.00
Fishwatching, $18.00

We offer many more books on hiking, walking, fishing and canoeing in New England, New York state, the mid-Atlantic states, and the Midwest—and many more books on travel, nature and other subjects.

Our books are available through bookstores, or they may be ordered directly from the publisher. For shipping and handling costs, to order, or for a complete catalog, please contact:

The Countryman Press, Inc.,
P.O. Box 175
Woodstock, VT   05091-0175
Our toll-free number: (800) 245-4151